D1727232

LEADERS AND MILLENNIALS

A Meeting Point of Generations

GUIDO STEIN

LEADERS AND MILLENNIALS
A MEETING POINT OF GENERATIONS

MIGUEL MARTÍN
(CONTRIBUTOR)

EDICIONES UNIVERSIDAD DE NAVARRA, S.A.
PAMPLONA

LIBROS IESE

Instituto de Estudios Superiores de la Empresa, IESE
Avda. Pearson, 21. Barcelona

First edition: 2019

© Copyright 2019. Guido Stein
Ediciones Universidad de Navarra, S.A. (EUNSA)
Campus Universitario • Universidad de Navarra • 31009 Pamplona • España
+34 948 25 68 50 • www.eunsa.es • eunsa@eunsa.es

ISBN: 978-84-313-3356-0
L. D. NA 287-2019

Impreso por Podiprint
Printed in Spain - Impreso en España

Except as permitted by law, no part of this work may be reproduced, distributed, made public or processed
without written permission of the copyright owners. Breach of the above terms may constitute an infringe-
ment of intellectual property rights (Articles 270 ff. of the Penal Code).

*To my son, Guido, who
lives out the bullfighter saying:
«No hay un quinto malo»*

*«What's important is not to be better,
rather to be good»*

Index

Prologue
From millennials to millennials

I would like to start by saying that I am not, nor do I pretend to be, an expert on the subject that this book is about, I am just a lucky person, belonging to the generation known as millennials, who fight every day to be better than the previous one. However, when Guido suggested that I write this prologue, in addition to filling me with pride, it immediately made me curious, and I thought, «What do I know about millennials?».

Like any other person in the world, I have spent my entire life with my own generation, but in the recent years (possibly months), here at the beginning of my professional career, I have begun to become aware of the great virtues (and «defects») of millennials.

It is a reality that we are impatient, therefore, we need to understand, and what should be explained to us as soon as possible, that certain things take time, «nine women do not make a baby in a month.» We are capable of pursuing very ambitious goals if we «believe in them», but we need help to be able to digest and handle that the frustrations are part of the journey. Maybe we seem a little arrogant because of our audacity, but the reality is that we value experience tremendously and, although it does not seem like it, we want to listen. Moreover, we need a lot of communication, since we appreciate and value the sincere and continuous feedback it helps us to grow every day.

We are curious by nature, and we like to encourage this curiosity, although from time to time it would not be a bad thing for someone to help us «hone in on the target» a little. However, it is not only about what we need rather what we can give as well. We are a generation that wants to show the world what we are capable of doing and we have internalized that the rules are meant to be broken and that is a definition of progress. Well focused, we are curious people that embrace meritocracy and like to learn new things and not just to earn more money. I have no doubt that with the help of those coming up behind us and especially from those who are already ahead, this generation will leave behind a very interesting chapter in the history of mankind.

A few months ago I began the deepest introspection process of my life, in which I am still immersed and which I am embracing and going through with the same enthusiasm and anxiety that I have always had. I felt lost. The constant comparing with other people and the feeling of «lack of emotion and meaning in life» that invaded me made me stop and reflect. I realized that something was not right, and decided that I needed help to get out of the cycle I had gotten myself into. These are some of the things I am learning, like that facing the frustrations is part of the path, and that the necessary and often essential thing is to «give yourself time».

In my case, it has also been a great discovery to leave behind the binary vision of success, something very common in the Hispanic culture. The success of others does not imply the failure of oneself; the reality is much richer and more complex. At the same time, I have stopped looking for «absolute truths» and I have begun to adopt less radical positions, without, of course, falling into relativism. Giving myself time to integrate what I think and what I feel, trying to empathize with the rest of the people around me is helping me to contemplate and integrate several points of view that enrich my vision.

My reflections are personal and may not reflect what happens to many readers of this book. What I do consider interesting in a general way, especially for my colleagues in the millennial generation, is to call for a sincere and profound reflection on ourselves. Our increasingly changing environment does not invite us to have clear the bases on which we will make the decisions that will mark our lives: what do I believe in and what not? What goals do I want to make? Am I who I would like to be? And an «etcetera» that each one of us has to personalize.

I have the intuition that many of us do not stop regularly enough to exercise healthy introspection, and if this prologue manages to make at least one millennial stop and ask himself the questions that he considers important, I will be satisfied. In the book you have in your hands you will find clues to focus the shot.

Nacho Vidri
26 years old, founder of Pompeii

Introduction

Categorizing people is not an easy task given the peculiarities and nontransferable traits of each individual. There are only ever specific people living in a particular era. Thus, when we refer to generations, we fall back on a generalization aimed at reflecting what specific individuals born during the same period have in common. This helps to group them since, as José Ortega y Gasset stated, «we're molded by the times in which we live,» especially during childhood and adolescence. While generalizations necessarily lack precise detail, they do help humans to think and communicate or, rather, better understand our nature.

The millennial generation encompasses individuals born between 1980 and 2000. They currently represent 32.8% of the world population, which translates to 2 billion people. Of these, 51 million live in Europe and 8 million in Spain.[1] In 2025, millennials will constitute 75% of the world's workforce.[2] Within this generation, it is possible to distinguish between senior and junior millennials.

Although the cutoffs between generations are somewhat vague, individuals born in the '80s are considered to be senior millennials. They were educated by parents belonging to Generation X or even the previ-

1. The Cocktail Analysis and Arena Media, *Observatorio Redes Sociales – Millennials*, 2016.
2. BBVA Innovation Center, *Millennial Generation*, Innovation Trends Series, 2015.

ous generation, the baby boomers. The education they received was very similar to that of their parents but they experienced a significant change with the sudden access to new technologies that allowed them to interact more intensely. The major technological milestones that marked that period include the increased use of cell phones and household Internet connections. Educated for a world that no longer exists, these individuals are too young to belong to Generation X yet too old to be considered junior millennials. Some have referred to them as «xennials,»[3] or people halfway between Generation Xers and millennials. They are the last generation that will remember what life was like before the Internet.

Junior millennials were born in the '90s. They were educated almost entirely by Generation Xers and grew up enjoying a high degree of independence. Given the absence of their parents at home and the access to new technologies they have had since a very young age, their education was vastly different from that which their parents received. They are often less well understood than previous generations and are often spoken about in cliché terms that mock their true profile. Members of this generation are considered digital natives and they show strong socialization via different online networks.[4]

Now that we have introduced the protagonists, let's continue on to the genesis of the book. The author has written this piece because of his need to better understand his own children, his students and the growing number of business professionals and directors with whom he works. As will be read later on, they are not different, rather they have mutated. What does this mutations consist of? What caused it? How can we keep up with it? Where is it headed?

Although the presence of the unexpected gives shape to the way we live, you can reduce the uncertainty that we cause through the full use of intelligence to understand things as they are (identify the truth) and decide what is best in each case (betting on goodness). Because of this enduring method, the years do not pass nor change the course of the generations, due do the fact that it has to do with what we are like as women and men since our creation. The author has interpreted it like the thread of Ariadne that helped Theseus out of the labyrinth of Crete before being devoured by the fearsome Minotaur. In this day and age, there is no Minotaur other than confusion.

---

3. A. Moreno (2017); D. Woodman (2017).

4. G. Stein, R. Mesa, and M. Martín, «The Leadership of Millennials: Profile of a Generation,» DPON-130-E, 2016; G. Stein, R. Mesa, and M. Martín, «Millenials, Work and the Company: Management Policies and Leadership Styles», DPON-131-E, 2016; G. Stein and M. Martín, «Millennials and Technology,» DPON-138-E, 2016.

The work is divided into three parts: the first is essentially descriptive; it addresses the common generational characteristics and their origin, giving special attention to the influence of technology on personal, social and business relationships, and it finishes with a set of reflections about how to direct them, and, consequently, how to be directed by them.

The second part shows three real cases which take a look at the convergence of the different existing generations, what happens within the scope of business organizations and the decisions and actions that should be adopted; in the third, the author gives his own perspective, which he has also weaved into the preceding pages, staking on a humanism that places the person on center stage, rather than a simulation of one.

I will begin this acknowledgment section with my research assistant and friend, Miguel Martín, whose collaboration in this intellectual and moral journey has made the experience infinitely more attractive and enriching. Rafael Mesa, a former student and expert manager, has collaborated on many of the pages, with special emphasis on those related to social networks and technology. Eduardo Rábago is the principal author of the American Valley case. Hundreds of students, businessmen and managers who have helped me as inspirers and critics must also be added to this short list.

To EUNSA, specifically to its editor, Esperanza Melero, for her cordial and effective professionalism.

To IESE, which has a preferential place on this list, and which has encouraged and facilitated the development of each line, the first publication of this piece as teaching material and its subsequent discussion, and which has benefited the final version now.

To my millennial children Jaime, Alicia and Luisa, and those who push them: José-Otto and Juan for having been a crucial part of the experiment. The fifth has already been metioned.

To Luisa, my wife, who has again chosen the title, the subtitle, the cover, and ..., I will stop here, because if not this list would be endless and too personal.

Madrid, December 2018
IESE Business School

Part One

Chapter 1
Profile of a Generation

They're not a new species;
they've just mutated to adapt to their environment

Millennials are a special generation (though perhaps every generation is special in one way or another) because, though by no means rev-
olutionary, they have been original in making it known that they're not
entirely pleased with the world we're leaving them. In the testimonies
we will present it is often clear that millennials go along with prevailing
social habits, such as those customary in companies, but do not make
concessions when it comes to what they believe is important, probably
because they hold out the hope of regaining a more worthwhile way of
life.

The way to manage people is to accept the traits that define them,
not to insist that they take on others deemed more suitable. Millennials
are what they are: normal but indispensable, worthy of respect and ad-
miration in many respects, though they also need to mature and be given
a push in many ways. Their virtues outweigh their faults, even though
they're immersed in a shifting fog created by the generation that preceded them, the materialism and selfishness of the world around them, and
the uncertainty that's part of the air they breathe. No generation has ever
had it so easy and so hard at the same time.

Those of us who belong to earlier generations share responsibility for their shortcomings, for the points where they need to be pressed more than for their strengths. This document is not intended simply to criticize: Our goal is to offer a straightforward analysis that serves as a call to action. In the next chapters we will take a look at the keys to attract their interest, motivate them and manage them.

A Generation Made Up of Micro-Generations

The term millennials is generally used to refer to people born after 1980 and before 2000. Some apply it only to those born after 1985; others use it only for people born in the 1990s. The philosopher José Ortega y Gasset said one generation gave way to the next every fifteen years. In fact, generations are becoming shorter and shorter because the environment they're raised in is changing ever more quickly as technological advances influence the way people live. In this note we will consider two micro-generations, which we'll refer to as senior millennials and junior millennials. This distinction is a helpful one when it comes to understanding their ideas, desires, needs, expectations and behaviors.

Those born between 1980 and 1990 can be classified as senior millennials. They are the younger children of parents born at the end of the baby boom, or the first born to Generation X parents. This micro-generation is distinguished by the fact that in the first years of their lives they were brought up the same way as Gen Xers, but this changed when certain new technologies, such as cell phones and the Internet, became part of their everyday lives. Members of this micro-generation feel like they've been brought up for a world that no longer exists. They're seen as too young to be part of their parents' generation and too old to keep pace with junior millennials when it comes to jumping on the new technologies bandwagon. They're caught between the authority of the «old guard» and younger subordinates quite unlike them.

Junior millennials are those born between 1990 and 2000. Some are the younger children of parents born at the tail end of the baby boom, but in most cases their parents are Gen Xers, characterized, among other things, by being very focused and absorbed in their work. In some ways the children of these Gen-X parents have developed and been brought up quite independently and differently from their parents. Access to technologies from a very early age is seen as one of their most significant defining characteristics. They're considered the first «digital natives» and feel very connected to so-called «social media.»

Regardless of any geographical or social distance that separates them, they're more alike than the members of other generations due to the uniformity of the information and values conveyed to them via new technologies. This could be seen as an effect of globalization.

What Are They like and What Matters to Them?

Our analysis will focus on junior millennials since they are the ones now starting to enter the labor market.

Family Environment

As we've already noted, junior millennials are aged 25 or under. Some of their parents were born at the end of the baby boom, but most are members of Generation X, notable for their competitiveness, individualism and independence, and for being impulsive consumers. Many of these Gen-X parents spend most of the day at work and frequently bring work home too. As a result, they're often absent from home in one way or another. Junior millennials got less attention from their parents when growing up than their predecessors did and spent more time in the care of grandparents or others, who in many cases didn't share their parents' values.

Their parents belong to the baby-boom generation, born in the period following two wars (the Spanish Civil War and World War II), and have been characterized by their austerity, patience and foresight. Members of this generation take a conservative approach to personal and professional decisions. Family usually takes precedence over work. Junior millennials have probably adopted some of their grandparents' beliefs, including, for instance, the idea that there are some things more important than work or success (though it looks like family isn't going to be one of their priorities).

On social media they show a strong attachment to their grandparents. There may be various explanations for this, but it suggests that junior millennials find in this earlier generation certain values they don't see in their parents. They've seen more clearly than previous generations what it means to have parents who are absent, work-oriented, and stressed-out due to job pressures. It's unsurprising, therefore, that many members of this generation are unsure whether it's such a good idea to make work the main focus of their lives.

Their World

The worldview of junior millennials has been shaped largely by the messages conveyed to them from an early age, first through television and later via the Internet and social media.

Lacking more immediate models, they've grown up paying attention to the patterns and values they encounter online, where they seek what they haven't found in their families or try to find alternatives to take the place of things about that milieu they don't like. Music stars, sports figures, YouTubers and other celebrities have known this from the start and constantly feed social media with content based on their private lives. They know their success depends on having a large number of followers and having a presence on communication forums.

As a result of these factors, junior millennials live in a world much more diverse than the one that existed in previous generations and find it much harder to make judgments based on absolute beliefs.

Influence of Social Networks

A social network is a structure made up of a set of actors who are connected in some way or have something in common. The social networks to which junior millennials belong are facilitated by social media based on technology and Internet access, and the most popular social media among this sector of the population include WhatsApp, Facebook, Instagram, Twitter and YouTube.

The relationship junior millennials have to these networks borders on addiction. They need to be constantly in contact with their social milieu. According to Telefónica's Global Millennial Survey, 83% of millennials believe they are on the cutting edge of technology when it comes to devices and applications, and 67% of those surveyed said they had accessed at least one social network on the day they were interviewed.

There has never been a generation whose members were so connected to each other. More than a network of friends, it is a living ecosystem that feels and reacts as a whole. Junior millennials use social media tools both to stay in contact with friends and acquaintances and to find new people. They probably know many people only superficially and only a few very well. The time people used to spend building strong relationships is now invested in reaching out to new people.

They're constantly taking the pulse of their personal relationships and their own popularity. As a result, they've become experts in crafting the image they project. But this ceaseless monitoring generates a level of anxiety and insecurity that was once uncommon in people of their age— feelings generated by the awareness that they're constantly being examined and judged by others whose acceptance they want.

This approval-seeking, driven by extreme digital proximity, proves stronger than modesty or shame; sex is trivialized («It's just another sport...») and loses its intimate, personal dimension; people of this generation see no reason to remain in a situation if there are no incentives for doing so, which means personal and employment relationships persist insofar as they're worth the effort (an attitude that translates into overt or latent selfishness).

At the age of 18, a member of this generation is likely to have tried most of the material experiences life offers. In certain areas, this leads them to feel disappointed, and that there's «not much left to discover.»

In the book Generation MySpace, Professor Candice Kelsey lists four messages young people absorb from social networking sites such as MySpace and Facebook:

1. I must be entertained all the time.
2. If you've got it, flaunt it.
3. Success means being a consumer.
4. Happiness is a glamorous adult (with «adult» defined primarily in terms of sexuality)

The teenagers with the most «friends» on social media are the ones who post the wildest stories and the most striking pictures or links. The «cooler» your profile, the more people will read it and send you friend requests, regardless of whether or not the picture it paints is accurate. The goal is to be recognized and have adoring fans.

A Way of Being

Junior millennials may come across as more self-centered and narcissistic than previous generations. They're addicted to public recognition and insist on being the center of attention. But they try to be agreeable and are eager to please, though at times they lack the self-restraint or experience required to avoid certain «digital conflicts» with those around them.

Members of this generation are somewhat immature because their socialization is incomplete. Social media help make it possible for them to stay in contact exclusively with their peers, from whom they receive hundreds and hundreds of impressions each day. This limits their exposure to people of other ages who are engaged in different activities. As Joel Stein writes, «17-year-olds never grow up if they're just hanging around other 17-year-olds.»

Junior millennials present a carefully crafted image through pictures and videos, which they use instead of verbal messages. Even at school, they made concept maps rather than the kind of outlines made by previous generations of students. This preference for images means they're more likely to use Instagram than other social media, in contrast to their senior counterparts, who tend to favor Twitter. Recently, a huge migration to Instagram has been observed.

They're impatient because their experience has taught them to expect instant responses. The social media they're hooked on have continuously and immediately delivered the inputs they constantly demand. Their philosophy can be summed up as «I see, hear, say, listen to, and do what I want, when I want to,» hence their dependence on technology. It's much more than just a pastime: They need constant and immediate stimuli and incentives.

This sustained habit of immediacy has made junior millennials comfortable with multitasking on various digital media. They fool around on WhatsApp and Snapchat while viewing Facebook posts, negotiating the purchase of secondhand clothes on Wallapop (see **Exhibit 1**), listening to their latest playlist on Spotify, or sharing their thoughts on last weekend's big game via Twitter—and still find time to check out the pictures their friends are posting on Instagram.

Though they can handle a variety of tasks, they may lack the ability to carry out in-depth analysis; and while they learn very fast, they seem to find it hard to develop real knowledge on their own. If you explain something to them, they get it right away, but they find it more difficult to think things through and reach the same conclusions for themselves. They've learned to take ideas in intuitively, but their ability to reason discursively is less developed.

Junior millennials are also exacting consumers who are used to receiving speedy, top-quality service. The tools and products they demand must be customizable to their own taste because it's important for them to convey a sense of uniqueness that makes them stand out against the backdrop of social media massification.

Their mastery of social media—and their understanding of the advantages and pitfalls they entail—has made them experts on networking. They're well aware of the collective force that lies behind social media and, with varying degrees of success, intuitively take whatever action is required to make these tools work for them.

Though drawn to material possessions, they're somewhat fickle and value experiences much more than tangible goods. Obviously, they need money and spend it, but their goal differs from that of the previous generation. They prefer to brag about their experiences than to show off their stuff—a predilection based on the belief that «It's not about what I have; it's about what I am.»

Consumption Habits

Millennials outnumber members of any other generation in history, including the baby boom. However, high rates of unemployment, falling wages and student loans (in the case of Anglo-Saxon countries) have left many with less disposable income than their predecessors.

According to a study carried out by Goldman Sachs in 2016, the percentage of young people aged 18-34 who live with their parents is now double what it was three decades ago. Though the average age at which people purchase a home has increased and millennials may start to overcome their reluctance to take this step when they reach the peak home-buying years (age 25 to 45). Ninety-three percent of people in this age group would like to buy a home at some point in their lives, but between 2005 and 2013 the number of millennials renting in the United States increased by more than 8%.

Another consequence of millennials' lower incomes is a growing tendency to access goods without buying them—what has become known as the «sharing economy.» The clearest example is cars. According to Jeremy Rifkin, «25 years from now, car sharing will be the norm, and car ownership an anomaly.» If goods can be used under a sharing arrangement, buying isn't a priority for this generation.

Millennials are also considered fast-moving consumers: They take a lot less time to make buying decisions than members of earlier generations. This is explained in part by the exponential increase in online purchases. No one should be surprised that a generation that spends much of the day online also shops online. This doesn't mean they take shopping lightly. On the contrary, they use all the information available to them online. And when they gather information, they trust other millennials more than brands or retailers.

In fact, millennials are loyal not to brands or products, but to the experiences they make possible, and they value these experiences more than the quality or functionality of the products they buy or the services they use.

Attitude Towards Authority

The notion of authority—at least as understood by earlier gener-ations—is foreign to junior millennials. They've grown up in homes where parents haven't exercised the same kind of authority they them-selves were subjected to when growing up, whether because they wanted to convey a different set of values or avoid conflict, or due to a lack of interest. Moreover, as children and teenagers junior millennials weren't subjected to strict discipline at school. We all know how hard it is for teachers to assert their authority in the classroom, and how common disobedience and inattention have become among younger students.

As the CEO of a leading multimedia group in the Hispanic world (born in the late 1940s) said, «I was brought up to be obedient and I obeyed, but I also learned that others had to obey me.» This is undoubt-edly one of the key points and greatest challenges when it comes to managing junior millennials, though it's not an issue, or at least less so, when dealing with those born between 1980 and 1990: Senior millennials understand authority because they were raised to live in their parents' world—a world that no longer exists. Some think this makes them inse-cure and nostalgic. A senior millennial enrolled in the IESE's executive MBA program said:

> «We grew up in the middle of the bubble, which burst just when we were entering the labor market, where we'd been promised that if we did as we were told (study hard and not waste time on the Internet and TV), we were going to take the world by storm. Now that we've reached the age when we're ready to actually do it, we can see that the people mak-ing big money are the ones who 'waste' their time on technology and TV. We're the last ones who studied under Spain's old education system (EGB and COU); it's a way of understanding the world that no longer exists.» (See **Exhibit 1**).

Junior millennials think their family members, teachers, and the peo-ple who manage them in the companies they work for don't understand them and, in particular, that they don't get the way they relate to other members of their generation through social media. They consider them-selves experts on these tools and tend to look on their superiors—who don't know how to use social media, or grasp their short-, medium- or long-term implications—with a degree of condescension. Clearly, the skill with which a «digital immigrant» navigates these environments is more limited than their own.

Digital Natives: Bibliophobia and Technophilia

Junior millennials have a knack for using technology. In addition to knowing everything their parents do, they can understand the genesis of a tool and predict how it will develop in the future because they can see the potential connections, advantages and disadvantages of each one.

One of the clearest consequences of being so focused on the screens of their devices, which they can barely tear themselves away from, is that to a large extent they've turned away from other, traditional means of acquiring and transmitting knowledge, including reading. The vast majority of junior millennials find reading unbearably tedious because it requires concentration and constant effort. Their ability to bring focused attention to a task is underdeveloped, and this affects the quality and depth of their thinking. Given their need to have their attention stimulated repeatedly, those who do develop a taste for reading generally prefer action-packed novels, in which they identify strongly with the protagonist (see **Exhibit 1**).

As a result of not reading much, they have a limited vocabulary, lack the ability to retain information, and have underdeveloped analytical skills. And to make matters worse, they have little interest in seeking to learn more (the less you read, the less you like to read). On the other hand, many junior millennials have outstanding qualities because the Internet provides them with the stimulus of fresh challenges, but there's little more to add on the plus side when it comes to the intellectual consequences of digital technology unaccompanied by training and study, as it will be addressed in the Third Part.

They have technological arsenals at their disposal and make the most of them. They create communities with millions of virtual inhabitants, have mastered the use of digital tools, and generate new approaches and techniques for thinking and personal expression. Through their digital immersion, they've redefined what it means to act.

In general, junior millennials are information managers, though those with talent become knowledge managers. Just accumulating data is no longer enough—they know how fast it changes—but some have managed to pull this information together rapidly, analyze it, channel it, and bring things into focus in a way that benefits their environment: «What's not used is sold on Wallapop and transformed.» It's a different way of seeing life.

Optimistic predictions about the incredible impact of a generation that's better educated and smarter thanks to digital learning, video games, high-tech classrooms, and all the powerful tools available online are yet to come true. Expectations for this generation may be higher than for any that came before and therefore more difficult to fulfill.

Relationship to Their Environment

«In the future everyone will be world-famous for 15 minutes»

Andy Warhol, 1968

Given their high level of interaction with many people in their environment whose personal circumstances they know very well, junior millennials accept sexual and ethnic differences much more readily than previous generations. They're not rebels or countercultural, among other reasons, because they don't have a single worldview, but float in multiple subcultures.

According to Joel Stein:

«They're earnest and optimistic. They embrace the system. They are pragmatic idealists, tinkerers more than dreamers, lifehackers.[1] Their world is so flat that they have no leaders [...]. They want new experiences, which are more important to them than material goods. They are cool and reserved and not all that passionate. They are informed but inactive [...]. They are pro-business. They're financially responsible [...]. They have less household and credit-card debt than any previous generation on record.»

They believe respect for differences is the highest value, so they don't rush to take sides. But this doesn't mean they're any less public-spirited than previous generations, since respect for others has increased within the culture as a whole. They're less involved in politics than previous generations, and since they were kids they've been hearing talk of the financial crisis, the housing bubble, political corruption, people living beyond their means, and so on. They have little faith in the political system, though they've begun to show an interest in changing it.

The fact that most of their interaction with people happens through screens may have weakened their ability to feel real empathy and deep concern for others. Consequently, despite their open-mindedness, they may struggle to understand different points of view. It's remarkable how

---

1. A lifehacker is someone who uses simple techniques to perform day-to-day tasks more effectively with the aim of being more productive, more motivated and happier. Being a lifehacker is a lifestyle.

effectively they can cooperate to make certain social events go viral (i.e. spread rapidly through social media)—though this doesn't necessarily mean they'll participate in the events they've helped publicize: Their attention may stray to other matters. The value they place on immediacy affects how they live and the choices they make.

They know their world depends largely on the image they project. It's therefore not surprising that the qualities they admire most in those around them are authenticity, consistency and humility. According to Telefónica's Global Millennial Survey, the issues they're most concerned about are the economy and poverty, and they see the shortcomings of the educational system and lack of political leadership as the main factors hindering growth.

They believe the education system is the main aspect of the country's infrastructure that the government should focus on, and they're critical of teachers and curricula. At the same time, they say good training is the key to their future success, especially if it's in programming and new technologies. Also, finding a good job is a higher priority for this group than buying a home or getting married.

Millennials have a lot to say and the rest of us have a lot of listening to do. In this technical note, we've tried to describe certain generational traits in order to better understand what we perhaps like least about them. We hope that these insights can be used to help them fulfill their true potential. In the final analysis, they're a generation of which we expect a great deal, and rightly so.

* * *

Millennials have a lot to say, and the rest, a lot to hear. In this chapter, we have tried to describe some generational traits that allow us to understand what we perhaps least like about them, in order to help them to become what they are called to be. In short, make up a generation in which there are high expectations, and rightly so.

EXHIBIT

Exhibit 1
Personal Aspirations of University and EMBA Students[2]

University Students: Personal Aspirations

1. To form a stable family, become a mother who passes on ethical values, and achieve happiness for both my family and myself.

2. To find happiness—balancing family, friends and work—and stay healthy.

3. To become a good person and help people. To be happy and make the people around me (in my life and work) happy.

4. To develop my abilities and achieve personal fulfillment so I can take good care of my family and help the people around me to the best of my ability.

5. To be an active and positive member of society; to grow as a professional and give something positive to the people around me, enhancing their lives through my positivity.

6. To learn to be a better person, maintaining a stable iife and a clear conscience, and be able to leave this world a bit better than I found it.

7. To feel, both in my work and personal life, that I've made a contribution and earned the respect of the people around me.

2. Based on surveys of junior millennials (the 50 top students in the most recent year at the University of Navarra's School of Economics and Business Administration) and senior millennials (120 IESE Executive MBA students), conducted in February 2016.

Executive MBA Students: Personal Aspirations

1. To be a father, in the short to medium term, travel with my family, and buy a home. In the long term, to be a good person; never (or almost never) to lose my way in life; to give my wife, children and family the best possible life; and not to pass through the lives of others without leaving some mark.

2. To form a structured family, to pass on to my children the values that have been transmitted to me (and give them the same opportunities I've had), and to be a good example to them and a very good husband to my wife.

3. To be someone whom the people closest to me can trust and rely on, and to mean a lot to them: support, understanding, a harmonious relationship, guidance and fun.

4. To strike a balance between my professional and personal life and avoid feeling I don't have a life of my own. To use the time from seven or eight in the evening till bedtime to be with my family or get some exercise.

5. To be of service, help others, be happy, and feel satisfied and proud of what I do; to take care of those around me and have a good balance in my personal life and my work; and to be able to afford the things that have always caught my fancy.

6. To learn to be a better person every day so my family and friends feel proud of me and can say that I'm someone worth knowing because of what I contribute to their lives and to society.

7. To reflect and apply my training, professional experience, and the support I've received from my family in my career so I can repay my family and friends for everything they've done for me.

8. To achieve balance in my life (wife, children, spirituality, etc.). To be confident that I'll always have time to spend with my family and friends.

Chapter 2

A Millenial Society

As pointed out, when talking about consumption habits, millennials rent more than their predecessor generations; their vital approach is different from that of earlier generations had: to become independent, to marry and to form a family. These are decisions that have been postponed. They want to enjoy their youth, so the entry into adulthood is delayed.

Delayed Matrurity

In surveys conducted at University of Navarra, it was observed that students between the ages of 20 and 24 left their homes at varying times. The youngest is 18, coinciding with the decision leave home to study a degree. Although taking this step is an important moment in terms of the personal maturity that they are beginning to acquire, they are still economically dependent on their parents, so it cannot really be considered a classic step in maturity.

The second time period to leave home occurs when the subjects are 22-years-old, when most of them have finished their studies and begin to work. At this time they are already financially independent, however, due to the precariousness of the job market, many of them have had to continue resorting to the subsidy of their parents.

The clearest moment to emancipate seems to occur from the age of 24, at which time more than 25% of them make the decision to pack. Those found at this peak are students who decided to take longer modules (engineering, medicine or double degrees among others) or those who continued their studies with the completion of a master, and professionals who decided to stay at home with their parents during the first years of working life, to be able to enjoy a comfortable mattress when it the comes time to break away from the family crest.

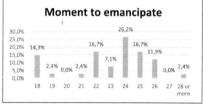

Source: Self-made.

40% of the polled millennials indicate 28 as the age at which they would like to get married. Personal and professional situations will determine the reality of the facts and we will see if their wishes are fulfilled or the average age of marriage is delayed.

Regarding the ideal age to have the first child, we observe the 30-30 phenomenon, where 30% of respondents view 30 years as the ideal time to conceive. If we look at the numbers in a cumulative way, almost 65% of them want to have their first child before they reach their 30th birthday.

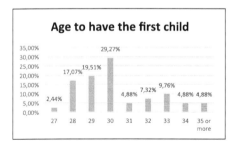

Source: Self-made.

The Second Adolescence

The adult generations are being infected by millennial behavior and are unexpectedly demonstrating it themselves. Generation X, those who should present the organization to millennials and serve as a liaison and mentor during their adaptation period are incorporating values of millennials in their own lives.

Instead of polishing the capabilities of millennials to fit in like pieces of a puzzle, there is a tendency to collect and adopt their behavior as their own and it is not surprising to find executives «runners» or «instagram ers», with different and not always desirable results, like a growing infantilism or immaturity among those who left adolescence years ago.

This visible millennialization of other generations is not necessarily negative, but it could weaken organizations, dispossessing them of values necessary for their proper functioning, such as respect for authority and leadership or the processes and rules necessary to coexist in a society. It is the same as if an orchestra director were to stop behaving as such and begin to adopt the behaviors of an instrument. This happens when the leaders of the organizations begin to adopt millennial priorities, styles and behaviors. Continuing with the musical simile, if a string instrument began to behave like a wind instrument, the logical and natural thing would be for the orchestra to lose its harmony. The same happens when the employees of generation X or postwar begin to behave like millennials.

One issue that arises in companies and social organizations is how to understand millennials and then direct them fully, and vice versa. In fact, younger managers often ask themselves: how do you address someone older than 40?

Chapter 3

A live overstepped by technology

While many millennials have already entered in the labor market, and the rest are knocking on the door of organizations, which have come to recognize a key consideration for managing millennials; namely, that they are a technological generation. In this chapter, we examine how technology affects the individuals who make up this generation and discuss some key points concerning how to lead a broadly talented generation.

A Technological Generation

Millennials in developed countries have grown up with technology. In other regions of the world, progress in this area has been slower but just as steady. As surprising as it may seem, globally, the average rate of internet access in 2015 was just 43% (see **Picture 1**). In the eurozone, however, the rate is 78.6%, slightly higher than in the United States (74%). Most of the remaining 20% of the population are probably members of older generations who, in the new world of the internet, have been less eager to learn how to use new tools. In this respect, they present a marked contrast to millennials, who have grown up in a world of constant change and technological development, to which they appear to have adapted without any difficulty.

PICTURE 1

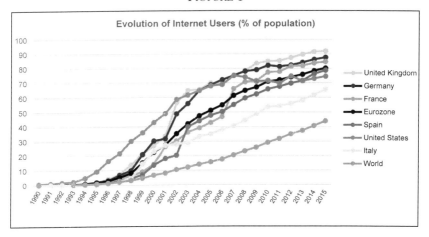

Source: Prepared by the authors based on World Bank data (https://data.worldbank.org/), last accessed May 2017.

In light of the data on internet access, Colbert, Yee and George (2016) point out that the focus is now on how young people, whom Prensky (2001) calls «digital natives,» use their access to the net. They are hooked on technology, and smartphones have become practically an extension of their bodies. When asked about his relationship to technology, a student of the University of Navarra's School of Economics and Business Administration replied, «If I'm not doing anything else, I'm constantly looking at my cellphone.»

Four years ago, at least 25% of young people said they used their smartphone or another electronic device within five minutes of waking up (Ipsos & Wikia, 2013). Today, that figure is close to 100% in developed countries. This is because young people have grown up with technology and used it to such an extent that they have become experts in this area. Moreover, having discovered the many ways in which it can improve their lives, young people have become true lovers and defenders of technology.

The importance of this tool for millennials is evidenced in the results of a study carried out by Cisco. According to *The Cisco Connected World Technology Report* (2011), a third of college students thought the internet was more important to the human condition than air, food, water or shelter.

Technology in Their Everyday Lives

The first way in which technology has clearly become part of the lives of millennials is as a tool for maintaining personal relationships: technological platforms connect people—at any time and wherever they are. Users connect to social media like Facebook, Twitter and Instagram, or use WhatsApp at any time of the day or night to communicate with both friends from school and coworkers, or to stay in touch with acquaintances who live outside the city or friends they have met while taking part in international experiences.

They also use social media to stay informed about current events and share their opinions, thoughts and experiences. In June 2011, the UN declared internet access a human right based on the understanding that it is a means of exercising the right to freedom of expression.[1] Thanks to technology, current generations enjoy greater access to information than their predecessors. The key issue now is distinguishing between high-quality and low-quality information.

Young people also use social media to follow companies they are interested in and observe how their friends work for them or access job vacancies. At the same time, organizations seeking to recruit young talent have a strong online presence (see Table 1).

TABLE 1
Online Positioning (number of followers)

	Twitter	Facebook
Google	17,500,000	22.349.043
BBVA	75,700	19.009.259
Mondelez	15,400	167.485
McKinsey	240,000	245.088
McDonald's	3,400,000	70.156.288

Source: Prepared by the authors based on the companies' profiles on their social media accounts.

1. CNNMéxico, «La ONU declara el acceso a Internet como un derecho humano,» *Expansión* (2011), http://expansion.mx/tecnologia/2011/06/08/la-onu-declara-el-acceso-a-Internet-como-un-derecho-humano?internal_source=PLAYLIST, accessed May 2017.

Gamification

The experience of millennials as children and adolescents has also been quite different from that of previous generations. While the latter would play outdoors with friends from the neighborhood and school, millennials have spent much more time inside their homes. In the warmth of their home environment, they had a TV to watch their favorite series and cartoons, and computers or video game consoles to play the latest popular games (alone or with friends). More recently, tablets and smartphones have been added to the array of entertainment options.

The use of games for the development of millennials and as one of their main forms of leisure has led to the coining of the term «gamification,» defined by Robson et al. (2015) as the application of game design principles to other contexts. According to Vinichenko et al. (2016), the main objectives of gamification in business are to increase motivation, create a climate that facilitates creativity and initiative, and increase employee involvement in learning processes (see Figure 1). These authors also note that the key factors that account for success in the application of gamification techniques are the creativity of the top management team (34.9%), having a young team (32.5%), and the creative activity of the company (28.6%).

FIGURE 2

Objectives of Gamification

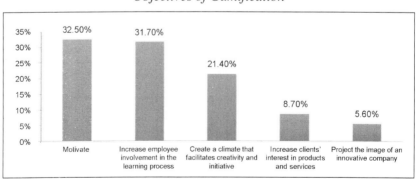

Source: Based on Mikhail V. Vinichenko et al., «Modern Views on the Gamification of Business,» *Journal of Internet Banking and Commerce* 21, no. 3 (2016).

Gartner (2011) notes that gamification has become a very popular strategy. Table 2 lists some of the many organizations that are using games or competitions, both internal and external, to attract, motivate and retain talent.

TABLE 2

Online Competitions to Attract Talent

Company	Competition
Peugeot	Talentos Marketing Peugeot: http://talentosmarketingpeugeot.com/
Deloitte	Social Callenge: https://www2.deloitte.com/es/es/pages/careers/articles/social-challenge.html
L'Oréal	L'Oréal Brandstorm: http://www.brandstorm.loreal.com/en/challenges/play-experiment-innovate
Google	*Online* Marketing Challenge: https://www.google.com/*online*challenge/
BBVA	Open Talent: https://www.centrodeinnovacionbbva.com/opentalent Outside the box: https://www.centrodeinnovacionbbva.com/opentalent/ideas

Source: Prepared by the authors based on information provided on corporate websites.

Video games have led to the development of modes of behavior and action that will be a significant factor in the personal and professional future of users. Brown and Martin (2015) emphasize that players have gotten used to learning through trial and error, an approach they identify as playing a key role in generating ideas and innovation in business activity. Glen, Suciu and Baughn (2014) point out that online games train users to take risks and learn from their mistakes, both of which are highly valued competencies in many current jobs.

Although a certain percentage of the respondents in our survey indicated they had not learned anything from playing video games, those who have spent the most hours engaged in this activity identified a series of skills they have developed through gaming. The main skills they mentioned were patience, motor skills, strategic planning, frustration control, money management, problem-solving through analysis of strengths and weaknesses, analytical skills, results orientation and decision-making.

The Digital Identity of Millennials

Increased use of technology affects the development and expression of a user's identity. Turkle (2015) points out that when people create avatars,[2] they often give them qualities that allow them to express aspects of themselves that they would like to explore. Whether they are writing a message or modifying their profile on a social media platform, users have the opportunity to create an aspirational image rather than projecting an authentic one.

No millennial who has given up their job to take up a position in London will use social media to comment on the loneliness they feel upon arriving in a new country or their frustration at not fulfilling their dreams. They will, however, emphasize how much they are enjoying the experience of having a coffee on a terrace in Soho. Those who read about their experiences will compare their contacts' prospects with their own everyday reality, although the virtual nature of the connection means that it lacks the intensity required to really understand the details of the situation. There is no substitute for physical proximity.

Gonzales and Hancock (2011) found that when participants in their study visited their own Facebook profiles their self-esteem was enhanced, probably due to the selective self-presentation that characterizes such profiles. It is therefore not surprising that authors often mention social media when they argue that millennials are more egocentric than other generations.

Despite of being specialists in taking care of their image on social networks, they make mistakes that recruiting experts claim should be taken more carefully. While being young, it is possible to make mistakes that in other generations went unnoticed and covered by the passage of time. On the contrary, today they are recorded on the web, since it is the millennials themselves who expose the view of society. Therefore, the new generations should be cautious and be aware of the danger of social networks.

Speaking with an international company HeadHunter, he told me one of his selection processes that frustrated him by being the perfect candidates for both skills, technical and social qualities and having the company already prepared the contract. The problem was that the president and CEO of the company, lover and defender

---

2. In the technology context, an «avatar» is a virtual identity chosen by a computer or video game user to represent him or herself on an application or website.

of the animals, entered by curiosity in the candidates Facebook and found a picture of him hunting. With this information he decided that he could not work hand in hand with him and had tu paralyze the process.

This is not an isolate event and many companies observe the online activity of the candidates before hiring them. They want to know what they think and how the candidates behave in their real life. The advice we have been able to rescue is that it seems that you have to be active, but without entering into political or personal judgments.

This generation is accustomed to receiving thousands of visual impacts, which reduces their ability to concentrate, increases multitasking, and makes it easier to influence them. Over 50% of the millennials we surveyed admit looking at their phone at least once every 15 minutes (see Figure 2). This clearly illustrates the tendency to multitask that is typical of a generation whose members cannot bear waiting to find out if they have received any messages from their friends.

Millennials have gotten used to dealing with constant interruptions while watching a movie at home or searching online for information they need to complete an assignment. Sixty percent of members of this generation receive over 100 messages a day, and 7%, over 500 (see Figure 3). They also reply to messages while at work, regardless of whether they are attending a conference or in the middle of writing a corporate report for their company.

Whether due to laziness, lack of interest or motivation, or the appearance of some new, more engaging stimulus, few read news stories or articles from start to finish; they take in only headlines and a couple of ideas highlighted in the text. The visual impact of publications that feature a lot of video footage or photographs is more effective when it comes to capturing the interest of this generation. This attitude reduces their ability to concentrate and analyze the reasons behind the things they read about or what is happening around them. Consequently, their ability to perform rigorous analysis is affected, which can lead them to make rather hasty decisions and often results in superficial thinking.

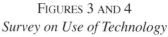

FIGURES 3 AND 4
Survey on Use of Technology

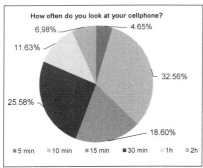 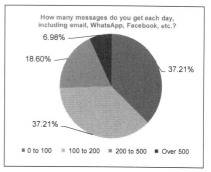

Source:Survey of students enrolled in the last two years of bachelor's degree programs in Economics, Business Administration and Management, and Law at the University of Navarra (academic year 2016/17).

Behrens (2009) notes that millennials are well-connected and aware of job opportunities, which makes it harder for companies to retain them than was the case in the past. Their idealized view of the external stimuli they receive, combined with their limited ability to engage in analysis, feeds their desire to pursue the better opportunities that they imagine they can achieve and feel they should already be enjoying—a mindset that makes it even harder for companies to retain them. Faced with a reality that falls short of their expectations, millennials can end up feeling frustrated, depressed or isolated, which often puts companies under more pressure to keep them motivated.

Effects on Work

Nass (2013) notes that young people regularly engage in various activities at the same time: they use social networks (checking Twitter, Facebook or Instagram, and exchanging messages on WhatsApp or Snapchat) while watching YouTube videos and listening to music on Spotify. At work, they behave in a similar way, so it is no surprise to find them using social media on the job.

New technologies facilitate constant conversation, but they also reduce the depth of our exchanges. According to Colbert, Yee and George (2016), «In texts or emails, we lose the ability to ask questions that do not have easy replies, to develop closeness, and to feel known and understood.» As a result, millennials can be less empathetic and find it harder to see things from the perspective of their coworkers. Authors such as Konrath et al. (2011) stress that increasing use of technology, especially social media, may be playing a significant role in the decline of real communication and, consequently, personal empathy.

On the one hand, technology makes it possible for employees to stay connected to work from home (Boswell & OlsonBuchanan, 2007; Perlow, 2012). On the other hand, 83% of them admit to using technology for personal matters at work (Cisco, 2008). However, in a more recent survey of students enrolled in the IESE Business School's Executive MBA program, the percentage of millennials who used social media for non-work purposes was slightly below 50% (much lower than was found in the Cisco study). For millennials, work and personal life are more intertwined than they are for other generations, and users tend to do what they think they should, whenever they see fit. Rigid office hours hold no appeal for millennials; on the contrary, they seek more flexible working arrangements that are more likely to make them feel at ease and happy.

FIGURE 5
Use of Social Media at Work

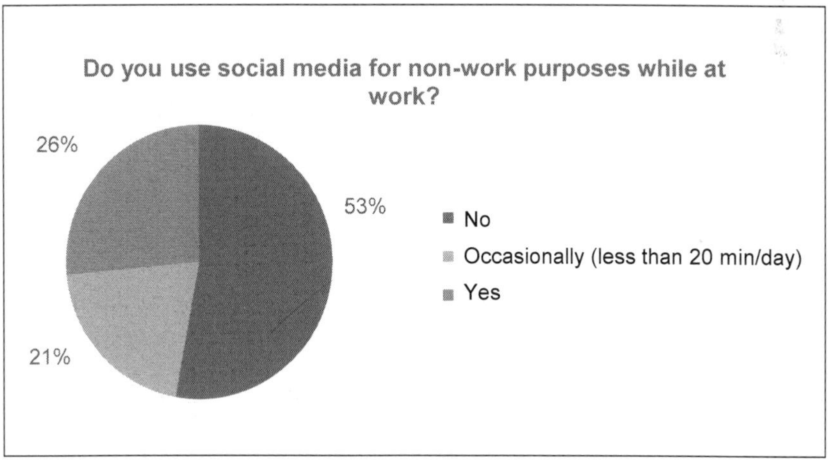

Source: Survey of Executive MBA students (2016) of the IESE Business School.

Although technology in the workplace is intended to make employees' day-to-day work easier, Barley, Meyerson and Grodal (2011) found that those who spend the most time dealing with email perceive higher levels of work overload. According to Perlow (2012), to avoid this problem, organizations like the Boston Consulting Group have granted their employees smartphone-free nights during the week. De Vita (2015) notes that some organizations are experimenting with technology-free meetings with the aim of improving communication.

Behrens (2009) and Cahil and Sedrak (2012), for their part, note that millennials expect to get everything right away. Technology has contributed to this attitude because it gives them immediate access to whatever they want, which encourages an attitude of impatience. In fact, 57% of users will close a web page if it has not loaded within three seconds. This craving for immediacy increases millennials' need for constant feedback and affects the way they perceive their career. They want to see progress right away, so they demand more work and attention from their superiors than the latter are used to receiving or demanding from preceding generations. «Apart from assigning me work and responsibilities, I'd like my boss to orient me, to mentor me and give me feedback»; «I'd like my boss to be a bit informal, to want to really teach me, and to make a real effort to help me learn. As well as telling me what I'm doing wrong, I'd like my boss to recognize my successes.» These were the answers given by two students of the School of Economics and Business Administration when, in the survey mentioned above, they were asked what kind of relationship they would like to have with their boss.

Millennials generally like working in teams. During their personal development, they have grown accustomed to this way of working in the context of sports activities, volunteer work and school assignments. In the workplace, they demand opportunities to use the same kind of approach. When asked what kind of relationship she would like to have with her coworkers, one student replied, «I'd like them to be friends, not too competitive — people I can ask for advice, and who make it easy and pleasant to work together.» These days, work teams are often geographically dispersed, but advances in technical solutions enable employees to work in virtual teams, facilitating collaboration, communication and transfer of documents (Gilson et al., 2015).

The training needs of millennials and their desire for independence give rise to a symbiosis that companies should not overlook. While earlier generations needed their companies to train them to deal with the problems they would face in their day-to-day work, millennials do not need this kind of training: when they need to use a new program or solve a problem they have never run into before, they just search online or watch a YouTube tutorial.

The Importance of the Internet and Social Media for Networking

One thing that appears to have remained constant with the passing of the years is the importance of building a wide network of contacts to achieve personal and professional success. If the doors of companies once opened more easily to candidates with recommendations from family members and acquaintances, something similar happens today.

The same social networking services that give people access to their idols also allow them to stay in touch with people they have met at one time or another. According to Professor Dunbar (2011), due to a cognitive limitation of the human brain, people can really only have four or five true friends. This is far fewer than the average number of «friends» users have on Facebook (150), and millennials have even more contacts of this kind.

While it is true that the traditional meaning of «friend» has been blurred in the social media context, millennials maintain virtual contact with hundreds of people (whether or not they are friends in the classical sense of the word). In the right circumstances, they would not hesitate to resume a real relationship with these contacts, whether to close deals between the companies they work for or to find a new position with another company. Because they stay connected with more people, they have direct knowledge of the reality of other organizations, so they find changing jobs less traumatic and even quite normal.

The Structure of Organizations

New communication technologies have made distance irrelevant. Millennials are used to having access to almost anyone at any time. Other generations also benefit from this kind of access but do not use it the way millennials do. Twitter, Snapchat, Instagram, Facebook and other social media have allowed them to communicate directly with their idols, who, recognizing the marketing and sales opportunities this generates, have opened their private lives up to fans.

Millennials also use this approach to communication, developed during their adolescence, in the workplace. If they do not get along with their boss or there is something bothering them, they will communicate this directly to their boss's superior, or even to the CEO or president of the company, often without thinking twice about the consequences.

This attitude is a source of quite a few conflicts. On the one hand, superiors see how they are being bypassed, and how their position and leadership are being called into question. On the other hand, the CEO's inbox is flooded with emails about subjects that do not really fall within their competence, though many senior managers like receiving messages of this kind and are even inclined to act on them. If a matter is of interest to the CEO, it should reach the top boss through the usual channels. This way, if the CEO deems it appropriate, they can go ahead and delve more deeply into the matter. Companies should establish mechanisms to counteract the disparity of perspectives that can result when the regular channels are bypassed. One important step is to ensure that direct superiors have a close and open relationship with the employees under their responsibility.

Maintaining a good relationship with their superiors and coworkers is so important for millennials that 40% of those interviewed said they would leave their job if they felt that such a relationship did not exist. One millennial said he would like to have a «close» relationship with his superior: «I'd like to feel there's enough trust that I can tell my boss about my concerns, and that they're proud of my work.»

Another defining trait of this new generation is their ability to manage change and take advantage of technological developments that allow them to move forward. The oldest millennials were born in the early days of computers, and by their late adolescence, all of them knew what a laptop and a smartphone were. The youngest were practically born with a smartphone in hand, and using apps is as natural as breathing for them. According to Deal et al. (2010), it is akin to learning a new language: people who have used technology from an early age attain a more advanced level than those who learn to use these tools later in life. Organizations should not ban millennials from using technology. This would be futile and counterproductive. The best approach is to encourage the proper use of such tools and offer guidance on how to use them in a smart way.

Bannon et al. (2011) explain that employers may be frustrated when they see an employee texting or surfing the net on their smartphone during a meeting. However, millennials are very skilled users of technology and may use their know-how to find answers to questions they are asked at such times. Furthermore, as Stein (2016) notes, over 56% would turn down a job in which they were denied access to social media.

Companies would be well advised not to put pointless restrictions on the use of technology and social media. In fact, they should take advantage of millennials' technological skill and orient it towards improving the competencies of the whole organization. One option would be to introduce reverse mentoring programs, as some pioneering companies are already doing. This way, millennials can help other employees or use them as sparring partners so they learn to better appreciate and make use of new technological developments and tools.

Accessible and Approachable Leadership

All companies need to ensure that the leadership function is fully exercised. This means giving direction to the people who make up a company and the tasks they perform so that all efforts are oriented towards the common good of those involved in the firm (employees, shareholders, suppliers, etc.) and the people it serves (customers and society as a whole).

Approaches to leadership vary according to the sector, the historical moment, and the particular character of each company, which results in part from the values and styles of its managers. To some extent, leadership is bound to reflect the needs of a particular time.

Millennials demand (and need) leaders who are accessible, approachable, warm and demanding. They know, and remind the rest of us, that there is no real substitute for personal relationships. Social media alone do not satisfy them as human beings or help them become better people.

Chapter 4
The impact of social networks

The Tools to Access Social Networks

Cell Phones

The world has gone entirely audiovisual and simplicity now prevails. We need only consider the launch of new technological devices to confirm such a statement: they offer an increasing number of features and are more and more intuitive to use. By combining several devices into one, the cell phone represents a comfortable, space-saving solution used by all generations. For young people, it can be argued that they have almost everything they need for their daily lives on their phones, as BBVA warns in its study entitle «How to connect with the Millennials».

According to the BBVA Innovation Center (2015) study, some 94% of millennials are smartphone users. Of these, 56% of women and 42% of men report being addicted to their smartphone.[7] Some 83% of millennials use their smartphone in bed, although this habit is shared by 46% of the previous generation (Lara and Naval, 2010).

The age at which people begin to use smartphones is getting younger. Before 2015, it was unusual for children under 12 to own a smartphone whereas nowadays that age has dropped to 10. It is now the go-to gift for those making their first communion (OCDE, 2015).

This increase in smartphone usage can be explained partly by the countless applications available on the market (both paid-for and free), thus making it possible to employ them for almost any purpose: instant messaging, social networks, online games, news and media, personal training, finances, etc. Around 34% of smartphone users also own a tablet. In general, tablets are used more recreationally and often at home, thus multiplying screen time.

As illustrated by the results of a survey completed by Tecnun[1] students who studied on the IESE program, the use of applications is so widespread among millennials that 46% of them use apps to learn or study for exams and 51% do so to look for employment.

Internet

Every day, 93% of US millennials use the Internet. They spend an average of three hours on weekdays and four and a half hours on weekends online. Some 22% report spending more than six hours online each day (Lara y Naval, 2010).

A survey completed by final-year Tecnun students yielded similar results: 21% of participants admitted to using the Internet for more than five hours daily, regardless of the day of the week (See Figure 1).

FIGURE 1
How Many Hours Do You Spend Online per Day?

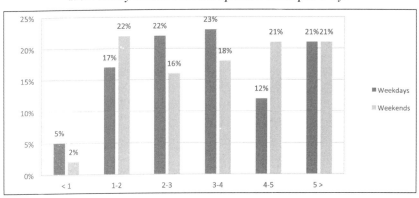

Source: Prepared by the authors.

1. School of Engineering of the University of Navarra.

Millennials are used to spending a great deal of time alone due to their parents' long workdays. While a TV made for the cheapest, easiest and most flexible babysitter on the market for the previous generation, the Internet and the different devices that connect to it, such as video-game consoles, have become the nannies of millennials (OCDE, 2015).

The amount of time millennials spend using the Internet and social networks has meant a decrease in TV consumption, among other things. It has been observed that, on average, people between 18 and 24 years old watch one hour less of TV per day than in recent years. They have a clear preference for a platform that grants unlimited access to any content, 24/7, from almost anywhere in the world (BBVA Innovation Center, 2015).

Results from the IESE survey of Tecnun millennials show that only 40% use a TV to access content, 53% use paid-for online platforms and 48% still admit to downloading pirated content. (See Figure 2).

FIGURE 2

What Platforms Do Millennials Use to Access Content?

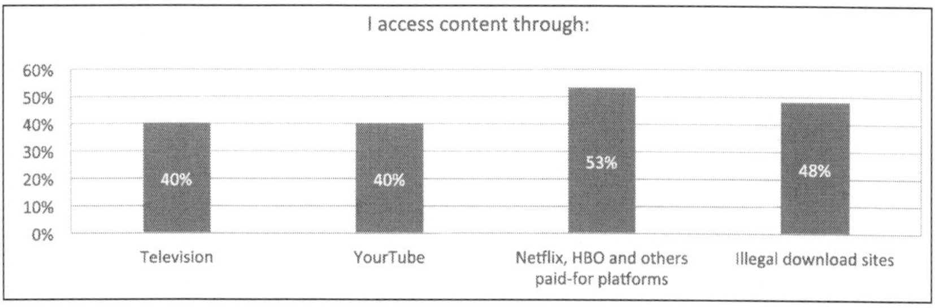

Source: Prepared by the authors.

Social Networks: What Are They and What Are They Used For?

A social network is a structure formed by a set of actors (such as individuals or organizations) that share a relationship based on certain criteria (profession, friendship, family, etc.). The first step to participating in a social network is to create a profile, which contains the image the user wishes to transmit to other members. There are two main reasons why people create profiles: to communicate and collaborate.

Firstly, there is a desire to communicate what one is thinking, feeling or doing and to discover what others are thinking, feeling and doing. People communicate their relationship status, just how exciting the sea-son-ending game was, vacation plans, job positions they have held over the previous five years, and an almost infinite list of other topics.

In addition to sharing personal information, there are users who create their own content beyond the bounds of their daily life, which they share because it contains knowledge, skills or experience valued by others. Content of this type might contain information about video games, recipes, IT tools, etc. People also use social networks to disclose their private lives, generate opinions or influence the behavior of others (such as their voting intention during elections or a contest) and modify them.

Along these lines, the second main reason why people create a profile on social networks is to kindle collaboration. Because social networks convert each individual into a separate communication channel, when users reach out to others they can influence and call on them to behave in a certain way, consume a given product, etc. That is why large companies and brands are contacting these influencers[2] in the hope of strengthening or expanding their image and business.

Likewise, social networks may also be used with the goal of achieving rapid mass collaboration, otherwise known as «going viral.» An example of using this process to a positive end would be a campaign to find organ donors, missing people or any other form of aid in general. An example using it for negative purposes would be for libel and slander, thus condemning individuals without a trial.

The great showroom of social networks is increasingly used as a place to Exchange and purchase new or used products.

But we must not forget that social networks, in all their uses, are based on user performance. A performance made through a complicated mechanism that we have been building between the act of exhibiting, and the desire to contemplate.

Main Social Networks

Some 95% of millennials have a profile on at least one social network and 49% confess to being addicted to them (Cambridge University Press and IPSOS, 2015). The most important ones are WhatsApp, Facebook, Instagram, Twitter and YouTube.

---

2. An influencer is a person with certain credibility on a given topic who, due to his or her presence and influence on social networks, could represent an interesting endorsement option for a brand.

WhatsApp

WhatsApp is a smartphone application used to send and receive messages over the Internet, thus complementing e-mail services, instant and multimedia messaging, and SMS. It is the communication method par excellence of both millennials and Generation Xers and is also widely used by baby boomers, even though they may not use all the functions that the tool offers. WhatsApp represents immediacy, constant stimulation and on-the-go consumption. It is used by 95% of millennials, of whom 90% report using it every day and 14% for more than three hours each day (Cambridge University Press and IPSOS, 2015).

Facebook

Facebook is the social network par excellence and «life itself,» according to its creators. It is a free online service that allows registered users to manage their own personal space where they can create photo albums, share videos, write notes, create events and share their thoughts and feelings with other Facebook users. Mainly used to share resources, thoughts and information with friends and family, Facebook can also serve to meet people or create a space to keep in touch with customers, among other things. It differs from other networks because there is a significant element of interactivity to it. There are miniapplications available, such as games, that make it easier to mix with other users. Some 84% of millennials use Facebook, 64% of whom do so on a daily basis (75% in the case of women) and 27% of whom log on less than once a week (The cocktail analysis and Arena Media, 2016).

When he left the company, Sean Parker, Facebook's first president, said he felt they were creating a platform that combined the persuasion techniques of advertising and the gambling industry to take advantage of certain character traits. For example, ads for betting houses would appear on the profiles of users for whom a potential gambling tendency had been detected. Moreover, he highlighted that many users were unaware that they were being sold to advertisers by unintentionally revealing certain traits and interests.

Finally, Facebook unveiled a massive study with 60 million users in which it showed that through its persuasive and publicity actions, it had been able to mobilize 340.000 abstentionists in the US elections.

YouTube

YouTube is a video-sharing website that hosts a wide variety of movie, TV show and music clips, as well as amateur content by video bloggers and gamers. It has become a very popular means of spreading Internet phenomena and promoting artists and politicians. YouTube is also the main platform for broadcasting a seemingly endless supply of viral videos that users find compelling for one reason or another—usually due to their humorous nature—and later share on other social networks so that more people watch them.

From this platform arose so-called YouTubers, who create their own content and post it periodically on their channels for all the world to see. Thanks to the large number of visits they receive, they charge for advertising. As for YouTube statistics, 81% of millennials check it at least once a week, while 44% do so on a daily basis: it is the TV on demand of this generation (Cambridge University Press and IPSOS, 2015).

Instagram

Instagram is a social network created with the main goal of sharing photographs and videos. Its users can apply effects such as filters, frames, warmth levels, contrast and retro colors and then publish their audiovisual content on Instagram or other networks, although Instagram is the most popular. It is considered the social network of choice for images due to the options available to edit photos and videos before sharing them. Moreover, it is focused on interaction exclusively through these formats and so the activities it offers are limited, although very efficient. Some 29% of men and 43% of women use Instagram every day and millennials use it 18% more than other generations (The cocktail analysis and Arena Media, 2016). It is the preferred social network of those born well into the 21st century.

According to a study by the Royal Society for Public Health and the University of Cambridge, Instagram is the application that most negatively affects the self-esteem of millennials. This is due not only to the recently detected fear of missing out on social events but also, and mainly, to users feeling that their lives or bodies are not sufficiently attractive or perfect. The technology available makes it possible to make almost limitless modifications to photographs, that to a large extent do not correspond with reality. Perhaps, from a palliative point of view, the solution is that the same application warns of which publications have been manipulated or that training campaigns are carried out on these risks in the school environment.

There are certain socially acceptable and very simple techniques employed to gain recognition on social networks, especially Instagram, so that anonymous users can gain levels of fame similar to or even greater than those enjoyed by celebrities in traditional media. They can be summarized as follows:

- Get people's attention quickly.
- Do not invent anything new but just copy what is already accepted.
- Give priority to photos with successful and established formats.
- Do not record for more than one minute.
- Smile.

Twitter

This social network is used to create short text messages containing a maximum of 280 characters (originally 140), which are shown on the user's home page. Members can subscribe to the tweets of others, which is known as «following» and is why we speak of «followers.» Messages are posted publicly by default but can also be sent privately and shown exclusively to certain followers.

This network is used most frequently to share personal experiences and points of view, follow live events, exchange opinions during such events, rebroadcast chats and talks that few people could access originally, and even comment on movies, TV shows and debates. Twitter is used by 48% of millennials, 38% of whom report using it every day (mostly men).[3]

The Impact of Using Social Networks

From observing how millennials use social networks, it becomes clear that they are moving progressively further away from those used by Generation X, to which their parents belong to a great extent, in preference for different ones. This makes Instagram, rather than Facebook or Twitter, the best way to reach millennials. Facebook is slowly losing users and connection time to newer social networks.

As mentioned, millennials tend to use networks with a greater focus on audiovisual content that can be edited and modified to their liking so

---

3. Cambridge University Press, and Ipsos. *Cambridge Monitor 3: Millennials en España*, 2015.

they can transmit the messages or images that best suit their purposes. They scrupulously avoid social networks that limit their behavior or restrict their interactions with others, as well as those that limit the level of privacy they wish to set for their publications.

When asked what matters most about a social network, the Tecnun millennials surveyed at IESE fundamentally mentioned four elements: the information and entertainment it provides; ease of use; immediacy and the possibility of staying in touch with long-distance friends; and privacy. They preferred a network that:

«Offers the option of privacy and allows me to be in control, so I can see the content I'm interested in.»

«Allows you to keep in touch with people who live far away. It must offer the possibility of accessing a large quantity of information quickly and easily.»

«Keeps me up-to-date about the activities of my 'friends' and is easy to use.»

Most influencers (see **Exhibit 3**) are millennials because they have understood how to use social networks to their advantage by mobilizing a large number of people through their content and becoming pioneers in monetizing their activity.

Regarding Technological Devices

Without the Internet, there would be no social networks, which is why millennials are hooked on networks that provide data and to the technology that allows them to process such data and translate them into virtual connection with others. They are relentless in their search for WiFi (Nielsen, 2014). They also have in-depth knowledge of the software and hardware of the electronic devices they use: smartphones, tablets, laptops, etc.

Moreover, they are also familiar with the best rates for phone and data plans available from all the operators on the market since, as shall be explained later, they are cautious consumers. They are also up-to-date on the potential functions of their devices via applications that can be downloaded. There is an almost infinite catalog of apps and the use of some has become a worldwide viral phenomenon.

In the Personal Sphere

Spending more time on social networks implies spending less time in the analog world, although this statement should be qualified. Sometimes, social networks are used with the goal of improving activities carried out in real life. For example, YouTube is used to perfect a specific recipe, Instagram to select an outfit and Twitter to find out what happened at the latest sporting event (OCDE, 2015).

Sometimes the opposite is the case: while carrying out activities in the analog world, people are interacting in the virtual world in parallel. For example, there are people who meet up with friends in person and, at the same time, participate in several WhatsApp conversations, upload information about their athletic performance to their social networks in real time, comment on Twitter about the shows they are watching on television, etc. The border between the real and virtual worlds is becoming more and more blurred (BBVA, 2016).

The hours spent on social networks are certainly the most «productive» if we consider interactions with a large number of people. However, it is worth questioning the quality of such relationships and the opportunity cost of having spent time exchanging bits instead of in a personal encounter.

The very way in which networks are configured makes interaction with other users more overwhelming: likes, new comments, status updates, direct messages, retweets, new tags, videos on the channels you follow, WhatsApp messages, etc. In the end, the amount of time dedicated to each person is actually not that much. Sometimes, users even feel as if they are playing a huge tennis match against dozens and dozens of other players and in which information if the only thing being exchanged.

While this type of activity promotes multitasking, it can also lead to a failure to learn from very useful mechanisms for social relationships, as well as a lack of real knowledge about the people with whom one is interacting.

As Chamath Palihapitiya (2017), a former Facebook executive, has pointed out, human interactions are being limited to hearts and thumbs-ups. Social networks exploit psychological vulnerability by creating a cycle of social validation feedback.

Of the millennials surveyed, 65% admit to using social networks while watching TV and 43% to doing so while in class or at work. Many survey participants also reported using the networks while traveling or using public transportation and some, being totally honest, admit to using them when bored.

FIGURE 3
When Do Millennials Use Social Networks?

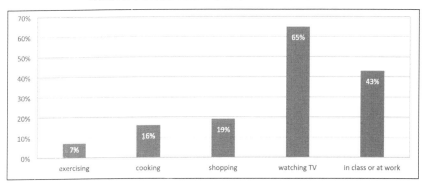

Source: Prepared by the authors.

Millennials show more symptoms of depression, anxiety and loneliness than previous generations (Twenge, J., 2017) since they feel the need to respond to this avalanche of information, although worse still is when they do not feel they have to because they are not popular enough. In some cases, this unpopularity can lead to bullying, which, despite it having always existed, can now even enter the home through mobile devices and social networks.

Millennials feel forced to prove at all times they are on the same level as others, at least socially speaking, which is why it is difficult to resist the temptation to brag about the «enviable» activities they do. Since it is a reciprocal habit, millennials know that others are observing their private lives, which leads them to take special care to display an idealized image of themselves that, at times, has little to do with reality.

For certain aspects of social relationships, which are usually not the most significant, millennials show a level of self-imposed standards that is unknown among previous generations. While individuals have always tried to meet certain social impositions, nowadays, social media are available to attempt to meet them 24/7.

Feelings of well-being and the amount of time spent on social networks are inversely correlated. Those connected to more networks suffer from greater anxiety than those who sign up for fewer. This is because the more networks one uses, the less expertise one has of them and, as a result, it is very difficult to achieve the desired results. Moreover, there is a greater chance of there being misunderstandings and of users feeling rejected. The dose of self-control required to avoid digital conflicts has grown exponentially.

Along these same lines, it has been revealed that people who stop using Facebook for a week feel happier and less anxious. The vast majority of individuals interviewed about social networks admit they would rather spend more time with their friends in person instead of via their cell phones (Twenge, J., 2017) but they continue to keep in touch digitally. Millennials represent the generation that interacts least with members of other generations, which may be one of the reasons why the period of adolescence is getting longer. This phenomenon is known as «extended adolescence» (BBVA, 2016).

Despite what one might think initially, millennials read more than previous generations, (Nielsen, 2014) just in a different way: nowadays, diagonal and headline reading prevail. In an attempt to optimize the monetization of their activity, the media have adapted to these) new trends by creating news stories designed to go viral. This is what the tyranny of clickbait[4] is about.

Such access to enormous amounts of data, news and commentary of all kinds promotes a combination of varied information and superficial knowledge, which establishes a positive correlation with manipulation — something that has come to be known as «post-truth.»

The algorithms that underpin the selection of content displayed to social network users take on great importance. In general, they are based on the history of each user and that person's preferences but they can be manipulated to show specific information.

In the best-case scenario, these algorithms do not show reality but learn over time and only present what users want to see, thus isolating them. In the worst-case scenario, they do not show reality because they display what others want people to see, thus manipulating them.

Along these lines, Chamath Palihapitiya (2017) points out that the behavior of individuals is being programmed without them realizing it. Taken to an extreme that is not far off, «bad actors can now manipulate large swaths of people to do anything you want».

Constantly launching superficial and easily digested messages designed to vitalize and reach as many people as possible. Social Networks are the most important tool for populist movements around the world, regardless of the political sign.

---

4. «Clickbait» is a neologism used in English to describe in a pejorative way online content aimed at generating income through advertising, especially at the expense of quality or precision, while relying on sensationalist headlines.

Through social networks, each person becomes a channel of communication that needs to let others know at all times how the user is feeling and what he or she is thinking. This affects the way millennials make decisions. They are losing their capacity for in-depth reasoning and are becoming mere transmitters of information. They are educated and prepared to absorb and learn intuitively, not to reason discursively. However, this has not posed any obstacles to becoming the greatest creators of content on the Internet.

Additionally, in some cases the habit of jumping from one activity to another makes it difficult to pay attention to arguments for an extended period or to listen at will. They require constant stimulus in order to keep their attention focused on any intellectual activities.

So much so that, as Susan Dynarski (2017) points out, on the basis of a study by Princeton University and the University of California, the use of electronic devices in class reduces the quality of content retention. When students take notes by hand, they are forced to condense the information they are receiving in their brains before expressing it on paper since they cannot write as quickly as the professor speaks, unlike what happens with electronic devices. Thus, the process enhances students' understanding of the topic.

Moreover, a certain increase has been noticed in the diagnosis of problems related to a lack of sleep. Intense activity in both the real and virtual worlds, together with the widespread habit (not just among millennials) of using mobile devices in bed to connect to social networks, is leading to a decrease in the average number of hours of sleep people are getting per day, as well as the quality thereof.

Another matter worth noting is that social networks are becoming transmitters of knowledge (Nielsen, 2014). This is important because millennials are the best-prepared generation in all of history and because information and its processing have become the raw material of the 21st century, with social networks being one of the most significant deposits. Millennials know that, with just a few clicks, they can access huge amounts of information and they understand that, more than possessing that information, the important thing is to know where it is and how to consult it. YouTube and Twitter are great tools for such purposes.

Lastly, it's worth pointing out that millennials have a great do-it-yourself ethos. They are «children of the crisis» and many are used to relying only on themselves and limited financial resources to achieve their goals. Social networks have helped in this regard, providing them with the knowledge, contacts and the mobilization of people required to meet their objectives.

As Members of a Group

Millennials are more aware than previous generations that they form part of a global community (BBVA, 2016), and that their actions affect others. They know both the power of a mobilized collective and how to achieve it.

Because millennials are continuously in contact, use the same sources of information and are affected, both in the real and virtual worlds, by the same phenomena, they resemble each other across the globe more so than any generation before them.

It is possible that in Spain this phenomenon is still developing because, generally speaking, the second generation of immigrants is still in its adolescence. On a global scale, however, and especially in developed countries, this daily communication with people from different cultures, both in the real world and online, makes them more tolerant and open (Twenge, J., 2017). They are accepting of racial diversity and do not attach so much importance to it as older generations did. They are used to managing cultural differences on a daily basis and have normalized them.

Nevertheless, they are more skeptical about politics and religion. They do not trust those in power. They feel more connected with their peers, even when they are culturally different, than with people higher up on the social ladder with whom they share a culture. In other words, they have an affinity that is more «horizontal» than «vertical.» They identify less with the concepts of «homeland» and «nation» and more with those belonging to their own generation.

Additionally, they are concerned about their impact on the world because they know that, to a greater or lesser extent, all global phenomena have ended up affecting them: the global financial crisis, housing bubbles, uprisings in other countries, the clear signs of climate change, etc. Therefore, millennials understand that their actions affect others. Social networks are the channel they use to try to make the changes they believe necessary (Nielsen, 2014).

Beyond just a group of friends, acquaintances and contacts, this interconnection has transformed this generation into a living ecosystem with a huge sense of belonging. There is also the important fact that their parents do not fully understand their habits or concerns since these deal with social networks, which their parents in general do not share.

This sort of generational isolation makes the need to be accepted by one's own almost an imperative, which is why they avoid the risk of being rejected, at least among those closest to them. Some 70% of millennials report that their friends are what matters most to them (BBVA, 2016). This might be another reason why their adolescence is lasting longer.

Bearing in mind that social networks can be considered their showcase in front of others, they take great care when creating and administering their profiles. They usually think about what image they wish to transmit ahead of time and then act accordingly. On most occasions, this image tends to be more aspirational than real. This has meant that the goal behind their publications and activities is often to show off or pretend rather than stay in touch with others, although ideally they would like to achieve both goals at the same time.

Millennials are experts at processing the images and facts they transmit and they measure their popularity through the reactions they provoke. They show greater knowledge of «personal marketing» than previous generations, at least within a virtual environment, although such skills can often end up being transferable to the real world as well.

This means that, to some extent, the messages they send and receive do not represent reality, or at least not with all its facets. When they do not reflect objectively on this fact, they are likely to feel jealous or envious when they see the activities or events occurring in the lives of others and not in their own. One might mistakenly think that, unlike everyone else, they are not achieving the life goals they have planned for themselves. This habit of publishing a segmented and idealized version of oneself merits in-depth analysis. Perhaps the reason behind its existence lies in the fact that millennials are not receiving all the attention, understanding and advice from the places where these were obtained traditionally.

This general lack of empathy from those closest to them leads millennials to channel the need to express their feelings through social networks and the people with whom they are in contact thanks to those networks. However, the scope of this channel admittedly may not be the most effective given the nuances that are lost in attempts to transmit such complex information through a somewhat limited means.

It is worth noting that feelings and ideas are given cardinal importance because they come from a person's most intimate side, so that neglecting them is considered offensive to the individual. The notion that we should respect human beings and not necessarily their ideas has become a thing of the past. Millennials offer the world their most vulnerable side but sometimes do not get the response for which they hope from others.

This «democratization» of the media has given a voice to many people who did not have one, which is why it is now possible to access a much greater variety of messages than in the past. There are undoubtedly many wise ideas and points of view but, on the other hand, there are people who flood social networks with publications or interactions that merely seek out recognition for being politically incorrect or for causing harm to individuals or institutions. Such people are known as trolls. Given the sensitive information that users display in their profiles, it is easy for trolls to find material for their activity, with the resulting collateral damage that their misdeeds cause for their targets.

The need to be heard and to achieve a certain relevance among one's contacts on social networks means that, to some extent, millennials battle daily for the attention of others. Therefore, the techniques they use may be quite similar to those of the professional media, such as giving their audience the most attractive content and publications in every sense, at the right time and in the right format.

They have developed «marketing strategies» that could be considered aggressive and, on many occasions, they resort to using their own bodies as bait. This means that certain social networks tend to display unnecessarily sexual content and there are voices being raised against sexist behavior. In a sense, it is paradoxical that some people who cry out against this sexism use the same tactics they are right to criticize to their own advantage.

Lastly, it must not be forgotten that the most intimate and personal relationships of this generation have been affected by the use of social networks. The trivialization of intimacy, together with the distance the networks provide, has, in many cases, led to a blurring of the notion of shame.

Topics of an intimate nature are now dealt with much greater ease. In general, sexual relationships no longer imply giving oneself to another person as they did in the past since they are now just another activity that can be carried out without negotiating commitment. Hence the «success» of some mobile apps designed to find partners to meet up with. Nevertheless, sexual encounters are still thought of more highly in the context of a stable loving relationship rather than outside of one.

At Work

It is important to realize that we are witnessing a process of professional transformation within the so-called «fourth Industrial Revolution» or «Industry 4.0.»[5] This transformation clearly has consequences for both how we work and how we understand work.

---

5. Industry 4.0 is a new way of organizing production methods. The intended goal is the implementation of a large number of «smart factories» with greater adaptability to the needs and processes of production, as well as a more efficient allocation of resources.

New professions are emerging, while others are disappearing and those that have lasted are being transformed. The vast majority of millennials who will be joining the labor market in the future will carry out activities that do not even exist today. Among the factors that affect the process of the emergence of new positions and the evolution of already existing ones, social networks play a very significant role. There have been pioneers who, as social network experts aware of the possibility of reaching many people, have discovered how to capitalize on their use of such networks, which is why figures such as YouTubers[6] or influencers have emerged. While it does not seem that this will be a feasible career option for the majority of the population, they do indicate the direction of trends in the use and importance of social networks in the world of work.

Both in private and professional life, using social networks to make oneself known or search for contacts and customers has become indispensable. Just look at the importance that LinkedIn[7] has gained in the lives of many people, the majority of whom are not millennials but Generation Xers or baby boomers.

The speed at which information travels through these social networks, regardless of its quality, as well as the reach that comments or opinions about companies and individuals can have make it absolutely necessary to project the right professional image. Millennials have mastered this thanks to their use of personal profiles and, moreover, they are open to modifying that image. They are flexible in this sense because they are used to asking and being asked, to interacting directly with companies and communicating with them without asking for permission (PwC, 2014).

Once a professional or company has signed up for a social network and decided what image they would like to portray to achieve financial and professional success, they have to determine the market niche they should focus on and, at the same time, establish what messages they will send, in what format and with what frequency.

The image chosen and the strategy to impact followers are very closely related. Both activities influence one another, and share a clear goal: to obtain a critical mass of followers who «consume» the content published

6. A YouTuber is a type of Internet celebrity who has gained fame through his or her videos on YouTube. «Some YouTube personalities have corporate sponsors who pay for product placement in their clips or production of online ads.»

7. LinkedIn is a social network focused on companies, businesses and employment. Based on the profile of each user, who openly discloses his or her work experience and skills in a genuine work résumé, the website puts millions of companies and employees in touch.

on the profile and who might be influenced by it. Millennials are experts at networking since they understand the advantages of collective power and know how to mobilize it.

Another point to consider is the role that work plays in the lives of millennials. While it represents a focal point for 25% of millennials, the percentage is 39% among baby boomers. However, millennials feel the need, more than ever before, to have their work recognized by their peers, friends and society in general and they use social networks to this end. In fact, «56% of millennials would reject a job position if it meant not being able to access social networks» (Michael Page, 2016).

Companies should be aware of these new customs and work to make social networks their ally. The use of such networks by their youngest employees can yield many benefits. Without going any further and to cite just one example, it can contribute to people establishing relationships with colleagues or potential colleagues within the same organization, whether it be in relation to purely professional matters or to common interests, thus enhancing visibility and internal networking.

Likewise, social networks can be used as an alternative way of spreading corporate culture and values, as well as to ensure that these are reaching all corners of the organization. They can also be useful in transferring these values to the world outside the company and in offering some of the recognition that millennials desire. Lastly, they help analyze certain trends and behaviors within the shared environment of employees and potential employees in order to find possible springboards and incentives to keep them motivated.

Nevertheless, social networks are sometimes a double-edged sword since they can become a channel through which negative aspects of daily life at the company are filtered to the outside world. Moreover, from the perspective of reputation and leadership, there is a risk posed by people with some degree of responsibility in the organization using them inappropriately. Thus, there should be a strong emphasis on preventing employees from carrying out certain actions and on them following the guidelines previously established to this end.

On the Market

Millennials know how to capitalize on their influence or rather how to retain the value created through shared content, views, interaction and impacts on the people they reach. Given the competition that exists on social networks and the relative ease with which content can be copied, a critical mass of followers is the most important factor.

Millennials are skilled at managing such plans, which may be new to those unfamiliar with the world of sales or marketing. They have grown up in a setting in which building an image, creating content (with high added value or otherwise) and obtaining a critical mass of followers have been commonplace actions for years. Evidently, this is influencing the coming labor market and will do so more and more. The questions worth asking in this context would be: What makes you stand out against the competition? How many people are you able to influence? How much do you make from it?

Mastering these techniques leads to knowledge of how to boost business through social networks or even outside of them. Some 72% of millennials believe that there are opportunities for them to become entrepreneurs. In fact, 50% of new entrepreneurs are millennials.[8] Social networks are an excellent catalyst in this sense because they promote networking between people in the same sector and access to technical and sales information as well as to suppliers and, above all, to customers, with whom they can keep in constant touch in order to study their behavior and, obviously, promote their services and goods.

In Spain, there are many examples of successful businesses led by millennials who base their way of operating on social networks: Hawkers, Pompeii, Mr. Boho, C21bebrave, etc. (See **Exhibit 4**.)

In Relation to Consumption

Nowadays, the greatest challenge for millennials is the strict financial control required to maintain their independent lives.[9] As previously mentioned, with them being «children of the crisis,» their debut on the labor market coincided, generally speaking, with the start of the recession. They have seen in their own homes the consequences of financial excesses and poor planning by their parents, companies and institutions, which is why they do not trust them and have grown up with the idea they can count only on their own means.

Consequently, they are cautious consumers (Nielsen, 2014) who search and compare opinions on the Internet about goods and services. In fact, 86% of millennials would stop buying from or doing business with a company due to poor opinions from other customers. They will

8. Telefónica. *Telefónica Global Millennial Survey: Global Results*, 2016.
9. BBVA Innovation Center, *Millennial Generation*, Innovation Trends Series, 2015.

not remain loyal to brands if these let them down and they trust information from other millennials much more than that provided by the brands. Friends and family are very influential in decisions on purchasing a product.

Nevertheless, this is not a consumerist generation in the strict sense of the word since, while there are obviously exceptions, millennials place greater value on experiences than on material goods: «It's not what I have. It's what I am.»

They do not need to own goods but only have access to them (access, not ownership), thus fueling the phenomenon of the the so-called sharing economy (Goldman Sachs, 2016). There are many examples of this nowadays: owning music in MP3 format has given way to listening to it on Spotify; buying a car has become renting it by the minute through car2go; buying new clothing has given way to exchanging it or getting it through Wallapop; reserving bus or train tickets has given way to sharing a vehicle through BlaBlaCar, etc. (See **Exhibit 5.**)

Such use of online applications has a disadvantage, which is that it is always necessary to provide personal data to access them. However, millennials are used to doing this since they do not give as much importance to privacy as previous generations. So much so that 66% of millennials would be willing to hand over their details to receive discounts.

This massive use of different tools and applications via various devices and channels makes it difficult to trace the origin of purchasing or consumption decisions despite the amount of information obtained through them, which is why advertising strategies to reach millennials are more complex than ever (BBVA Innovation Center, 2015).

Final Thoughts

The use of social networks has allowed millennials to be more open to changes in the surroundings, show greater tolerance and empathy regarding different values and cultures and constantly share experiences, knowledge, tastes and entertainment with people from the whole world since they know they are affected by the same things in a very similar fashion.

They have a more analytical and global view of business and companies than previous generations, which are more traditional and focused, at least initially, on local markets. Millennials are more careful financially speaking because they have witnessed the disastrous consequences of excess in this regard since childhood. Their way of learning and dealing with tasks and activities is different from that of their parents. Among other things, they better tolerate multitasking.

Generally speaking, they have developed a greater artistic concern and aesthetic sensitivity than previous generations since they have had unlimited access to limitless and free quantities of content for as long as they can remember. This has allowed them to shape their tastes in a more sophisticated and demanding way than in past decades. However, as the use of social networks has spread throughout this generation, a series of challenges has emerged, which they must face to develop their social, psychological and emotional conditions and skills properly.

Social networks make it possible to access huge amounts of information about oneself and others. Nevertheless, it would seem that, in general, the chance to access such information is of no use for boosting personal growth or self-awareness or, consequently, maturity. In fact, while it is true that personal contact has been improved both in speed and frequency, people now show levels of anxiety and feelings of loneliness never before recorded.

Millennials are not alone. In many cases, they can rely on people from the previous two generations to provide a more experienced view of events and accompany them closely and responsibly in the process of overcoming the challenges they face. In turn, younger people can simultaneously provide support to older generations in a reverse process, in taking advantage of the positive aspects offered by social networks.

EXHIBIT

EXHIBIT 1
Key Data for Each Generation

	Baby boomers	*Generation Xers*	*Millennials*
Approximate age	*From 51 to 69*	*From 35 to 50*	*From 16 to 34*
% of world population	16%	21%	30%
Core values	Anything is possible Equal rights and opportunities Personal growth	Entrepreneurship and pragmatism Skeptics Search for a balanced life	Self-assurance Part of a global community Experts in technology
Consumption	Travel Health High-end cars Pension plans Grandchildren	Children Real estate Family cars Financial investments Cosmetics	Technology Education Travel Leisure Well-being
Most-admired brands	Sony Toyota Levi's Procter & Gamble Kodak	Microsoft Mercedes Ralph Lauren Coca-Cola Philips	Apple Audi Zara Starbucks Google

Source: Prepared by the authors.

EXHIBIT 2

Key Statistics on Millennials' Use of Social Networks

%	Concept
95%	have a profile on at least one social network
95%	use WhatsApp
94%	have a smartphone
93%	use the Internet daily
90%	use WhatsApp daily
84%	have a Facebook account
83%	use their smartphone in bed
81%	visit YouTube at least once a week
75%	of women use Facebook daily
64%	use Facebook daily
56%	of women say they could not live without a smartphone
48%	have a Twitter account
44%	visit YouTube daily
43%	of women use Instagram daily
42%	of men say they could not live without a smartphone
41%	say they could not live without using social networks
38%	use Twitter daily
34%	have a smartphone and a tablet
29%	of men use Instagram daily
27%	use Facebook at least once a week
22%	spend more than six hours using the Internet each day
16%	do not have a Facebook account
14%	spend more than three hours using WhatsApp each day
6%	do not have a smartphone
5%	do not have a profile on any social network

Source: Prepared by the authors.

EXHIBIT 3

Prominent Influencers in Spain

Social network	Name	Description	Profile
Instagram	Gala González	Fashion posts. Considered the most important fashion blogger in Spain.	@galagonzalez
Instagram	Dulceida	Fashion posts. Received the European award for the Best Style Fashion Blog at Berlin Fashion Week.	@dulceida
Instagram	Herrejón	Posts about the daily life of a millennial.	@hersimmar
Instagram	María Pombo	Posts about the world of fashion and personal experiences.	@mariapombo
Instagram	Grace Villarreal	Posts about makeup: product reviews and looks inspired by female fashion celebrities.	@gracyvillareal
Twitter	Norcoreano [North Korean]	A parody account about the North Korean dictator Kim Jong-un.	@norcoreano
Twitter	Señorita Puri	An account that talks about a mother's routine and the different situations she faces each day.	@SenoritaPuri
Twitter	La vecina rubia [The blonde neighbor]	An account that talks about current affairs in fashion, style and other diverse experiences from a humorous angle.	@lavecinarubia
Twitter	Bebi	A humorous account that posts comments, reflections and recommendations about how to deal with certain aspects of personal life.	@srtabebi
Twitter	John McClane	An account that comically reflects on experiences widely shared by members of the millennial generation.	@john_mcclane
YouTube	El Rubius	A channel that posts gameplays, practical jokes, viral challenges, commentary on personal experiences and collaborations with other YouTubers.	elrubiusOMG
YouTube	Vegetta777	A channel that posts gameplays for newly released or soon-to-be-released video games and comments very personally and swiftly on the process of both individual and multiplayer rounds.	VEGETTA777

Social net-work	Name	Description	Profile
YouTube	AuronPlay	A channel that posts practical jokes and commentary on personal experiences and other YouTube profiles from a humorous angle.	AuronPlay
YouTube	Patry Jordan	A beauty channel that posts step-by-step explanations for different hairstyles: updos, half updos, braids, buns, ponytails, DIY, hair accessories, etc.	Patry Jordan
YouTube	Marta Riumbau	A channel that posts recommendations and more personal experiences about fashion, decoration, recipes, trips and lifestyle.	Marta Riumbau

Source: Prepared by the authors.

EXHIBIT 4

Spanish Companies Led by Millennials

Name	Description	Link
Hawkers	Online sales of sunglasses. Started in 2013.	www.hawkersco.com
Pompeii	Online sales of customized sneakers. Started in 2014.	www.pompeiibrand.com
Mr. Boho	Online sales of customizable sunglasses, watches and other accessories. Started in 2013.	mrboho.com
Muroexe	Online sales of sneakers with a functional design based on user experience. Started in 2014.	es.muroexe.com
C21bebrave	Online sales of customizable sunglasses, watches and other accessories. Special emphasis on combining fashion and values. Started in 2013.	www.c21bebrave.com
Auara	Bottling company whose dividends go toward water-extraction facilities in developing countries. Started in 2013.	auara.org
Luxmetique	Manufacturing and distribution of nutricosmetic products. Started in 2016.	luxmetique.com
We are knitters	Online sales of knitting kits. Started in 2011.	www.weareknitters.es

Source: Prepared by the authors.

EXHIBIT 5

Key Applications in the Sharing Economy

Name	Activity	Link
Netflix	US entertainment commercial enterprise that, through a monthly flat fee, provides multimedia streaming on demand via the Internet (mainly movies and TV series), as well as DVDs sent via Permit Reply Mail. Netflix was founded in 1997 and its headquarters are located in Los Gatos, California. It began operating as a subscription-based service in 1999.	www.netflix.com/
Spotify	Multiplatform application used to stream music. It uses a freemium business model, meaning it offers a basic service with advertising to which features can be added, such as better audio quality, via a paid subscription. People can listen in radio mode, searching by album, playlists created by other users or artist name. The application first went into use on October 7, 2008, in Europe and it was launched in other countries in 2009.	https://www.spotify.com/
Airbnb	Software platform and company whose name is shortened from «AirBed & Breakfast,» which offers accommodation to private and business tourists. Between its launch in November 2008 and June 2012, 10 million bookings were made via Airbnb. It has approximately 2 million properties on offer in 192 countries and 33,000 cities.	https://www.airbnb.com/
Tinder	Tinder is an application that allows users to connect with other people through geolocation to chat and plan dates based on their preferences. It was launched in August 2012.	tinder.com
BlaBlaCar	BlaBlaCar is a French car-sharing services that makes it possible for users going to the same place at the same time to travel together. In doing so, they share fuel and toll expenses and avoid excess emissions of harmful gases.	www.blablacar.com
Car2go	Car2go is a subsidiary of Daimler AG that provides a decentralized car-rental service in European and North American cities. Customers use an application to find the nearest car and they can unlock the door using the application or a card. Moreover, users can reserve a vehicle up to 20 minutes beforehand without this counting as rental time.	www.car2go.com
Wallapop	Spanish company founded in 2013 with a website for the purchase and sale of second-hand products, aimed at being used on smartphones. It uses geolocation so that users can buy and sell based on geographic proximity.	es.wallapop.com

Source: Prepared by the authors.

Chapter 5

An organization for millennials

While millennials account for 34% of the workforce in the United States (see **Figure 1**) —and that percentage is on the rise— current workplace structures are tailored to previous generations, which leads to generational conflict and the loss of motivation among millennials. This chapter is focused on examining that dispute, as well as how such structures can be adapted to make them compatible with the preferences of new generations.

FIGURE 1

Generations in the Workforce

Generation	Age in 2015	Percentage of the US workforce
Silent generation	70+	2%
Baby boomers	51-70	29%
Generation X	35-50	34%
Millennials or Generation Y	18-34	34%
Postmillennials or Generation Z	< 18	1%

Source: Deborah Hopen and James J. Rooney, «Do Generational Differences Affect Project Success?,» *Six Sigma Forum Magazine* 15, no. 3 (May 2016).

Ambidextrous or Versatile

Scott (2014, 44) argues that «the ability to compete in current and new markets begins with the strategies and priorities that are responsible for the very nature of innovation capabilities.» It is not on the market where an organization starts to become competitive, by offering different products and services to end consumers, but during recruitment of the talent that will design and develop such products and services to be placed on the market. Thus, the innovation process within organizations should start from the human resource (HR) department, with new talent-recruitment policies adapted to a generation with different traits and wishes. Ferri-Reed (2014, 13) suggested that employers need to transition «from a 'boomer-centric' workplace to a 'millennial-centric' workplace.»

Birkinshaw and Gibson (2004) identified a strong positive correlation between business performance and ambidextrous organizations. If we apply this to the HR department, we could argue that a company that focuses its talent-recruitment and retention policies on current and future employees will achieve better business performance, as well as better financial results. Nowadays, many companies still have policies designed for baby boomers and Generation Xers and have not yet modified them for those just starting out in the business world—that is, millennials and postmillennials. Since they will be the ones holding job positions in the future, those in charge of designing and applying said policies should pay attention to their demands and wishes, with the goal of achieving a more ambidextrous organization.

With new generations comes the energy of those first entering the workforce, marked by a desire to get work done and prove their worth in the short term but also by inexperience regarding the business world and the internal history of the company. However, they possess almost innate technological knowledge and can operate technologies with enviable ease. Therefore, the need for knowledge transfer between generations (Calo 2008; Hewlett et al. 2009; McNichols 2010; Helm-Stevens 2010) has become bidirectional, such that establishing reverse mentoring programs can be useful. This need within organizations for employees to share their knowledge is complemented by millennials' wish to receive constant feedback (Gibson et al. 2009; Patterson 2005; Thompson and Gregory 2012). In a survey conducted at IESE, 65% of students reported having asked for feedback (see **Figure 2**) and explained that they did so to understand where they were making mistakes and how to improve and make important decisions. Parents, professors and friends are crucially important in providing this feedback. (See **Figure 3**.) When these students take on job positions, their bosses will take on the role of their professors.

FIGURE 2
Do You Often Ask for Feedback?

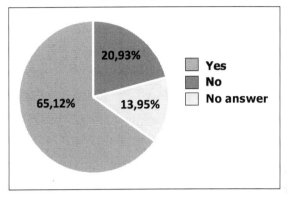

Source: Prepared by the authors using data from the survey of students of the University of Navarra's Faculty of Economics who were studying on the 2017 IESE Program.

FIGURE 3
From Whom Do You Usually Ask for Feedback?

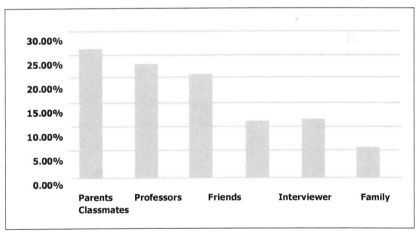

Source: Prepared by the authors using data from the survey of students of the University of Navarra's Faculty of Economics who were studying on the 2017 IESE Program.

To adapt to new generations, business leaders are modernizing their policies with flexible work schedules, whereby employees work 24/7 without having to go to the office. This results in the intertwining of their personal and professional lives. Promotion policies, feedback and the implementation of reverse mentoring programs are also changing to adapt to new generations (Bannon et al. 2011; Chaudhuri and Ghosh 2012). These and other authors argue that a good first step for many organizations that aim to become more innovative would be to build a model with a strong emphasis on promoting knowledge transfer while producing a generational replacement.

The Organization

As explained in the technical note by Lavezzolo and Rodríguez-Lluesma (2015), an organization can have one of three types of structure: functional, divisional and matrix. In the first case, the division of labor, the roles and the hierarchies are structured in terms of the activities or primary functions that the organization must perform when carrying out its business activity (production, sales, engineering, finances, etc.). This type of structure is very clear and maximizes individual functions. However, in doing so, it can hinder the maximization of the organization's overall outcome. The second type of structure rests upon the things produced, geographic markets or customers. It is suitable for highly uncertain settings in which the goal is to coordinate innovation, satisfy customers and retain a market segment.

As for the matrix structure, it attempts to combine the features of the previous two structures, thus benefiting from their positive aspects while seeking to avoid their drawbacks. In this structure, two or more dimensions are defined through the implementation of a dual management system with responsibilities assigned to functional departments, in which division and functional managers have the same authority within the company and employees depend hierarchically on both. This structure is especially recommended when a company must respond to two sectors simultaneously, operates in very uncertain and complex settings, needs to innovate or has to cope with tough restrictions on human and financial resources by making use of economies of scale.

Regardless of the organization's structure, and given the differences that exist among millennials with regard to their behavior, it would seem they need help understanding and adapting to company rules. Moreover, their need for achievement and instant gratification makes reviewing and monitoring their expectations vital in many companies. Their motivation to understand how companies operate along with companies' interest in paying them due attention mean that dual management—through two supervisors—might promote their integration and company retention.

Corporate Culture

When it comes to running a company, either a hard- or soft-power culture of corporate governance can be established. The first option entails strict rules, whereas soft power alludes to the subtle mechanisms of culture as effective instruments for changing organizations. As we shall see, soft power allows managers to make the necessary changes while causing as little friction as possible, avoiding collateral damage and earning the cooperation and consent of the other members of the company. In short, it creates a viral effect in their governance program. Low-intensity norms are a useful instrument for cultural transformation because of their flexibility and their ease of implementation.

However, at times, the urgency of business activity or the existence of a strong culture makes it hard to implement long-term changes, forcing executives to make quick decisions with immediate effect. Strong cultures, which can be modified only through reactive changes, also have some advantages, such as increased motivation, coordination and control. Moreover, they put companies in a better position to respond to investment opportunities and, generally speaking, help to consolidate competitive advantages. Nevertheless, their rigidity often makes it harder to implement soft changes.

The basic features of corporate culture are very well defined by the kind of organization the company has decided to implement. Some theoreticians have tried to explain how organizations work based on the following three models:

- **Mechanical models:** The organization is viewed as a technical system and its members as mere economic agents. They simply reflect the scaffolding of the company's formal organization. At the same time, the influence of the true organization, or corporate culture, is underestimated. These are companies whose main goal is to maximize profit, in which people act as parts within a mechanized productive system, and the prime incentive to encourage improvement is economic reward—that is, extrinsic motivation.

- **Organic models:** The company is articulated as a living organism whose members deliberately depend on each other. While the mechanical model is restricted to defining the productive and remuneration systems, the organic model tries not only to maximize profitability through economic efficiency criteria but also to satisfy the current motivations of the organization's members. It includes the basic features of any technical system, yet it strives to transcend practical, measurable usefulness. The company is thus viewed as a living, social organism in which different individual preferences have to be coordinated, and some may even be at odds with each other at times.

- **Anthropological models:** The organization resembles an institution and the people are the core of the business activity. Firstly, it puts individuals at the heart of managerial activity and their real motivations become the main goal of the business strategy. Secondly, the company is viewed as an institution with its own specific values, whose mission is to relieve society, other companies, families and individuals from the functions it performs. While institutionalizing cultural values, anthropological organizations prioritize satisfying the transcendent motivations of their members.

Theory of Motivation

When people act, they can be driven by three kinds of motivation (see **Figure 4**):

- **Intrinsic:** The result of the action benefits the person carrying it out solely through the act of performing it (for example, lessons learned from it or the pleasure of doing it).
- **Extrinsic:** The incentive comes from a person or people other than the person performing the action (for example, payment for work or praise received after performing it).
- **Transcendental:** The result of the action benefits people other than the person performing the action (for example, when a mother satisfies a child's hunger or when you help out a colleague at work).

FIGURE 4
Theory of Motivation

Source: Juan Antonio Pérez López, *Fundamentos de la Dirección de Empresas* (Madrid: Rialp Ediciones, 1993).

Culture Focused on Innovation

Hershatter and Epstein (2010) point out that, compared to Generation Xers, a significantly greater number of millennials prefer to work at organizations with centralized decision making, clearly defined responsibilities and official rules and processes. In line with this data, Kaifi et al. (2012) discovered that millennials opt for an organizational culture with few rules and regulations. Moreover, Behrens (2009) found that millennials require a more structured organization in which they are told what to do and when to do it. Based on these studies, we can conclude that millennials prefer fewer but clearly defined rules.

Innovation is becoming increasingly more important to the success of organizations, given the technological changes occurring in all sectors of the economy. Moon (2014) found that organizational cultures that promote creativity and passion and that value their employees will become leaders in innovation. Similarly, Martensen and Dahlgaard (1999) stated that, to build a successful culture of innovation, workers must be encouraged to learn, and leaders must commit to examining how they are improving products. Millennials highlight continuous training and learning as fundamental requirements for staying at a job or deciding to take a different one. As can be seen in **Figure 5**, 25% of millennials surveyed cite learning as their main reason for working, while another 22% refer to personal development—which, of course, cannot exist without learning. Therefore, offering continuous training should be among companies' main concerns.

De Jong and Den Hartog (2007) explain that a culture of innovation is based on task autonomy or, rather, on the ability of the workers in charge of creating innovative ideas to choose how they complete their tasks and, in doing so, to feel supported in their decisions. This study would support the idea that companies that want to adapt to market currents and new generations should establish few rules and give their employees a certain degree of autonomy, with the goal of structuring their work and generating innovation. In this sense, support for their decisions and ideas is a necessary feature of the organization's new models since another important trait of millennials is their need to feel supported and valued within their company. In this regard, Burstein (2013) points out that millennials require companies to be open to receiving and listening to comments and criticism.

In this new order of relationships in the organization, the preestablished hierarchic rigidity is pushed aside, making way for atmospheres in which open dialogue can flourish.

FIGURE 5
Why Do You Want to Work?

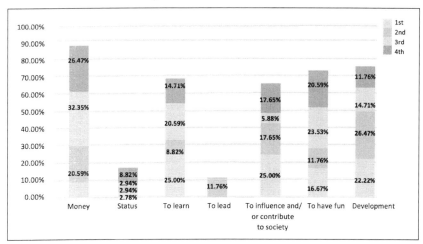

Source: Prepared by the authors using data from the survey of students of the University of Navarra's Faculty of Economics who were studying on the 2017 IESE Program.

Corporate Social Responsibility (CSR)

New generations give increasingly greater importance to the content of their work. In fact, money now ranks fifth as the main reason why millennials choose a job, behind metrics such as «to learn,» «to influence and/or contribute to society,» «development,» and «to have fun.» (See Figure 5.) However, money still occupies a position of capital importance since almost 90% of survey participants report it as one of their four main reasons for working, while less than 80% are interested in personal development. Our survey obtained the same results as a study by De Hauw and De Vos (2010), who argue that the significance of a job and the enjoyment thereof are more important than earnings. Moreover, they confirm that millennials prefer challenging jobs that can help them advance in their careers. Therefore, it comes as no surprise that many of them opt for jobs at the smallest companies, where they believe they will be able to perform a more practical role and have a greater impact (Caraher 2015).

Companies have not given much consideration to this aspect of work until now, which is why the incorporation of millennials into the workforce may lead to an increase in employee turnover, as millennials find they do not feel passionate about their job or stimulated by it (Skowronski 2012). For their part, De Hauw and De Vos (2010) and Kowske et al.

(2010) include as a reason for the high turnover of millennials the fact that, because of the economic recession, this generation's sense of job security has declined.

Likewise, millennials seek out teamwork and stay in close contact and communication with their supervisors, from whom they demand intense feedback (Gürsoy et al. 2008; Martin 2005). Accustomed to playing team sports and working on group projects at school, it is no surprise that they opt for this type of organization in their professional lives rather than individual work. Their supervisors need to be in constant contact with them, not just because millennials demand it but also because, through fluid communication with them, it is possible to gather significant information about how to manage and motivate them and keep them at the company.

In this sense, a company department that is gaining special importance is the one in charge of corporate social responsibility (CSR) since, as Bannon et al. (2011) point out, working for an organization that helps people has become a priority for the millennial generation. Similarly, Winograd and Hais (2014) maintain that this is the only priority that takes account of employees who are searching actively for CSR opportunities and who work in an environmentally friendly way. Therefore, organizations that want to create a setting that leads to a greater retention of millennials should carry out CSR activities.

Teamwork

As previously mentioned and as argued by Cahill and Sedrak (2012), millennials have developed the capacity for working in groups and they place greater value on teamwork. This is primarily due to a shift in teaching methods, whereby students' progress is no longer evaluated by a final exam but through continuous work carried out in groups. Social networks also play a role in millennials placing greater value on teamwork rather than individual work.

Good relationships with colleagues and supervisors are very important to millennials, as 50% of survey participants cite poor relationships with colleagues as one of the three main reasons for changing jobs and more than 40% include a poor relationship with their boss among those reasons. (See **Figure 6.**)

FIGURE 6

What Would Incite You to Change Job?

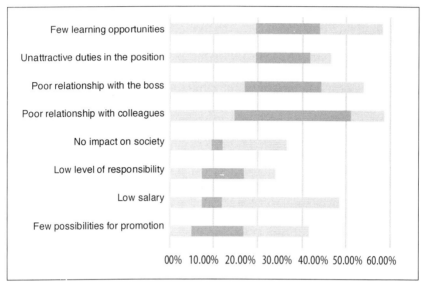

Source: Prepared by the authors using data from the survey of students of the University of Navarra's Faculty of Economics who were studying on the 2017 IESE Program.

In fact, Myers and Sadaghiani (2010) believe that millennials will know how to interpret their colleagues' opinions and will make an effort to show their true value. In the interviews conducted, millennials mention they want to work with people who are «friends, who are not very competitive, from whom you can ask for advice and with whom it is easy and pleasant to work.» They also hope for «a collaborative and friendly environment in addition to a working relationship» and «a great deal of camaraderie» and they want «some colleagues to become friends» and «everyone to help each other mutually.»

Attract and Retain: «Professional Career»

The generations preceding the millennials experienced a childhood in which affection and education were wrapped in an iron fist both at home and at school, where they listened and obeyed without complaint. Nowadays, this style of education has given way to more lenient authority. This difference in the educational development of millennials means that management of them at organizations should be different. Andert (2011) points out millennials' preference for an interpersonal relationship with their supervisors, in which they know their managers are concerned about them. Likewise, she highlights that, while ambition is the most highly valued characteristic of baby boomers and Generation Xers, millennials prefer a boss who will look out for them.

Our survey participants did not hesitate when defining the type of relationship they hope to have with their superiors: «A relaxed relationship with a lot of learning, where I feel like they want to teach me»; «In addition to giving me work and responsibilities, I want my boss to guide me and offer mentoring and feedback»; «A bit informal, where my supervisor truly wants to teach me and makes an effort so that I learn. I would like my boss not just to tell me where I make mistakes but to recognize my achievements»; «A close, trusting relationship, so I can tell the boss my concerns and for the boss to be proud of my work»; «Mutual trust, with respect, not a buddy relationship, but for them to be concerned about me and ensure I learn, for them to challenge me.»

As maintained by Tulgan (2009), adaptation must be bidirectional, in which millennials and organizations work together to meet the needs of both parties. Managers should be responsible for ensuring the success of this process, insisting that millennials meet the company's standards while, at the same time, making sure the company fulfills their desires.

Thompson and Gregory (2012) point out that the relationship with immediate supervisors might be key in order to benefit from, motivate and retain millennials. They are the ones who accompany them during their daily activities, which puts them in charge of picking up on their worries and keeping them active while balancing their dreams and expectations with reality. For a generation willing to change jobs, the soft skills and empathy of managers are becoming more and more important.

Recruitment and Retention: The Importance of a «Professional Career»

A study by PwC, the University of Southern California and London Business School (2013) shows that the reasons for staying with or leaving a company are practically the same for all generations, although the reasons' order of importance in their final decision varies. According to the study, millennials have greater expectations of being supported and appreciated in exchange for their contribution and for forming part of a team. Therefore, it is necessary to review the characteristic traits of each generation to establish work motivation policies. In fact, research shows that, compared to Generation Xers and baby boomers, millennials place greater importance on being challenged at the workplace (Gibson et al. 2009) and on mentoring and continuous training (De Hauw and De Vos 2010).

Murphy et al. (2010) and Kaifi et al. (2012) argue that managers should learn more about the work satisfaction and organizational commitment levels of their employees as new generations join those already present in the workplace. Similarly, Guha (2010) maintains that, to attract and retain millennials, it is necessary to understand what motivates and satisfies this generation. According to Tapscott (2009), to this end, Microsoft has a private lake, 25 cafeterias, and American football, baseball, soccer and volleyball fields at its headquarters in Seattle, Washington.

To explain the changes occurring within companies when it comes to seeking, recruiting and retaining talent from new generations, Rexrode (2016) mentions Citigroup's plans. «I want people to have family lives, personal lives,» said the CEO of Citigroup, while his company announced quicker paths to promotion, opportunities for charity work and the possibility of working on microfinance projects in Kenya for four weeks, as part of its plan to recruit and motivate the youngest employees in the organization. Likewise, Rexrode points out that entities such as Goldman Sachs, Bank of America and JPMorgan Chase & Co. are planning similar changes in order to recruit millennials through more interesting job tasks, charity activities and quicker promotions.

Super (1970) distinguishes several stages in a professional career. The first stage, in which Millennials are found, is considered to be exploration. Individuals make choices for their career by «trial and error» and if they are not satisfied with their choices they make new explorations or adjustments. Once satisfied, the individuals begin to stabilize and the efforts dedicated previously to exploration are dedicated to self-development in the chosen field. The problem that arises for organizations, is that millennials have concerns and expectations in their exploration, often difficult to achieve. Therefore, they are considered as a more given to the change and rotation of posts generation. In this sense, organizations that wish to retain talent in their organizations could propose rotation programs, where millennials face problems, activities and challenges in different departments of the organization. In the next chapter, we will return to this central issue.

Day-to-Day Experience: Real Policies of Organizations

To prepare this section, we have researched the selection processes of several companies and collected information about human resource goals and policies from the annual reports of large companies.

The selection processes of companies interested in recruiting young talent are evolving. Gamification plays a significant role in this change and many companies are considering contests in which the winner receives a grant or internship. This allows companies to hire talent they have previously appraised through the simulation of work experience and the resolution of problems similar to those that people must face at the organization on a daily basis.

With the goal of developing new employees quickly and making them feel appreciated within the company, many organizations have implemented graduate programs. Most of these programs consist of a period of between one and three years of rotation through the different departments or positions within departments.

Below are the main human resource policies of large companies such as Google, Facebook, LinkedIn, Yahoo and Amazon. (See **Figure 7**.) It is worth noting that some general principles are shared by most companies, such as alignment with the business strategy, pay for performance, recruitment and retention of the best talent, as well as external competitiveness.

FIGURE 7

General Principles of Human Resource Departments

Google (2015)	• Attract and retain the world's best talent. • Support Google's culture of innovation and performance. • Align employee and stockholder interests. • Pay Googlers competitively compared to other opportunities they might have in the market. • Believe deeply in paying for performance.
Facebook (2015)	• Attract the top talent in our leadership positions and motivate our executives to deliver the highest level of individual and team impact and results. • Encourage our executives to model the important aspects of our culture, which include moving fast, being bold, communicating openly, focusing on impact, and building real value in the world. • Ensure each one of our named executive officers receives a total compensation package that encourages his or her long-term retention. • Reward high levels of performance with commensurate levels of compensation. • Align the interests of our executives with those of our stockholders in the overall success of Facebook by emphasizing long-term incentives.

LinkedIn (2014)	• Support, attract and retain the best talent. • Support a high-performance culture by rewarding excellence and achievement. • Recognize and retain top-performing talent via differentiated rewards and opportunities; reinforce alignment with our Company's values (in particular, a focus on excellence and an attitude of ownership). • Create alignment with our Company's long-term performance. • Provide an opportunity for each employee to share in the success we create together.
Yahoo! (2015)	• Recruit great talent to build the next generation of products that will grow revenue, and build shareholder value over the long term. • Motivate and retain that talent by developing compensation packages that reward performance in a manner the Compensation Committee believes is responsible and in line with market norms. • Deliver the majority of executive compensation in stock to align the long-term interests of management with our shareholders.
Amazon (2015)	• Attract and retain the highest caliber employees by providing above industry-average compensation assuming stock price performance. • Provide strong long-term incentives to align our employees' interests with our shareholders' interests. • Emphasize performance and potential to contribute to our long-term success as a basis for compensation increases, as opposed to rewarding solely for length of service. • Reinforces and reflects our core values, including customer obsession, innovation, bias for action, acting like owners and thinking long term, a high hiring bar, and frugality.

Source: Prepared by the authors based on the companies' annual reports or proxy statements.

Chapter 6

Millennials, Work and the Company

In this chapter we describe the attitude of the generation that recently entered the labor market, sum up the key points to bear in mind when adapting traditional management policies to this new reality, and identify the management styles needed to deal with younger employees.

When millennials began entering the labor market, members of Generation X received them with skepticism, and baby boomers were no more welcoming, perhaps because of the natural tendency to maintain a certain distance and respond cautiously to what is unfamiliar.

Members of these two previous generations generally didn't think about what companies could offer them, but when millennials arrived on the scene, firms were forced to consider what steps they could take to reduce unwanted turnover or loss of employees. For younger employees, compensation packages, deferred compensation and career plans are no substitute for rewarding day-to-day work (see **Exhibit 1**, which reflects the results of a series of surveys on the professional aspirations of junior and senior millennials[1]).

1. Based on surveys of junior millennials (last year's top 50 students at the University of Navarra's School of Economics and Business Administration) and senior millennials (120 IESE Executive MBA students), conducted in February 2016.

Figure 1 shows the priorities of junior millennials when it comes to choosing a job, and Figure 2, those of senior millennials.

FIGURE 1

Junior Millennials and Senior Millennials

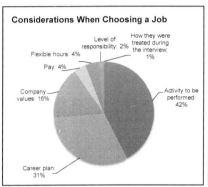
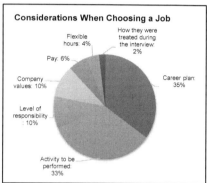

Source: Prepared by the authors.

According to «The 2016 Deloitte Millennial Survey: Winning over the next generation of leaders,» certain factors have more influence on decision-making for department heads who are senior millennials than for those who are junior millennials. The factors in question are personal and company values, the progress of the company, impact on customers, achieving objectives, avoiding trouble, and impact on colleagues. Broadly speaking, these are the same factors that would have guided members of the previous generation, Generation X. However, senior millennials are on the same page as their junior peers when it comes to the increasing importance they place on work-life balance and participation in decision-making. It's also worth noting that there is less rivalry or competition between members of different generations than there is between employees of the same age.

The impact of these generational traits on the labor market and on the day-to-day activity of companies is already evident. There has never been such a wide gap between leaders and those led. A junior millennial resembles another member of their generation on the other side of the world more than their boss, even if the latter lives in the same neighborhood they do.

Junior millennials often don't understand their superiors, and as it has already been said, they see no reason not to bypass them and tell senior management what's on their minds. They're convinced they have the right to do so. This kind of behavior reflects a lack of awareness that's largely the result of them not seeing the point of authority and never having been «punished» to remedy this fault. They're like the youngest siblings in a large family whose parents were too worn-out to correct their behavior.

Leaders need to work closely with millennials to encourage and guide them. At the same time, they should avoid setting themselves up as models or flaunting their authority. The degree to which junior millennials accept their bosses will depend on the latter's professional standing and the consistency of their actions.

How Millennials See Work

For junior millennials, it's very important to perform tasks that engage them (that are «cool») and to feel they're part of an important project that contributes to making the environment around them a better place. The world that's taken shape doesn't (and cannot) give them a sense of fulfillment, so they need to get this from the tasks they perform—to belong to organizations that give them a sense of purpose and meaning. Junior millennials need strong organizational cultures, and they need to be motivated by goals they believe in, that draw them out and get them to give best of themselves. In a sense, the company is a place where they can continue the human dimension of their education as well as honing their professional skills (even if they're not really aware of this).

They have to see the results of their work close-up and be recognized and rewarded for their performance. They also need to share the tasks they're working on and their successes with friends and their network of contacts. They therefore need external recognition for their work and to see evidence that the effort they've made has been worth it. Junior millennials have a stronger need than members of other generations to feel a sense of belonging, and that they're part of an engaging project. Teamwork and cooperation are also more important to them.

As a result of these specific psychological needs, the use of technology and social media at work is vital for members of this generation. Their work, which is naturally an important part of their everyday lives, serves as a tool for conveying the image of themselves they want to project. They want to show people how they dress at work, what means of transport they use to get there, what the tasks they perform involve, the people they meet, the trips they make, and so on—all with the aim of ensuring that this information contributes to the impression others form of them.

If junior millennials can't engage in actions of this kind in the job they have—whether because the tasks they perform or the environment they work in doesn't fit with the image they want to convey, or because they don't have free access to social media—they'll probably end up looking for another position that allows them to satisfy this need. In fact, 56% of millennials say they'd refuse a job in which they were denied access to social media.[2]

To draw an analogy, if the dishes served in a new restaurant targeting millennials weren't eye-catching enough to be photographed and allow patrons to show off what they were eating, the establishment probably wouldn't have much of a future with this generation. They seem to expect frequent promotions and recognition, even if it's not necessarily as a result of them taking on greater responsibility. This is partly because they aren't confident that their superiors are aware of their accomplishments.

The relationship between millennials and baby boomers—who place more value on work, believe productivity takes precedence over leisure, and recognize the hierarchy inside a company—can play a valuable role in orienting members of the younger generation and helping them learn how organizations work. At the same time, both baby boomers and Gen Xers have a lot to learn from the newcomers, who are eager to show their older colleagues the reach of new technologies and how these tools are transforming the markets everyone wants to gain access to.

How to Lead Millennials

Figure 3 sums up human resource policies in six sections, and in Figure 4 we list ten critical factors for millennials. In this section we will relate HR policies to the key factors outlined in the second table in a highly practical way.

2. Michael Page. «Millennials: Friend or foe?» http://www.michaelpage.ch/employer-centre/attraction-and-recruitment-advice/millennials-friend-or-foe, accessed April 2016.

FIGURE 3

HR Policies

Policies	Keys to Implementation
Hiring and Recruitment	• Objectively determine short- and medium-term staffing needs. • Design a management system that identifies the required knowledge and skills for a given position. • Nourish and reinforce the company brand by strengthening relations between the marketing, communications and HR departments.
Onboarding and Integration Process	• Monitor the onboarding of new hires, integrating and training them from the outset. • Designate appropriate mentors and guides for new hires.
Development and Training	• Treat training program attendees as customers, taking care of every detail of the process. • Know the level of knowledge and skills of the organization's personnel. • Define, share and communicate the performance evaluation system with each participant in the training process. • Assess the returns on training without being slaves to metrics.
Evaluation and Promotion	• Don't lose sight of the organization's culture and values. • Align the implementation of evaluation systems with development systems. • Establish transition periods during which the evaluated person will have time to make the necessary changes in accordance with the information gathered.
Compensation	• Define the career development model prior to implementing a compensation scheme. • Make sure schemes and salary levels are internally and externally consistent. • Define the relationship between the evaluation and compensation systems.
Internal Communication	• Be aware that communication also takes place through policies and management styles. • Be creative in identifying communication channels. • Bear in mind that the most impactful communication flows informally. • Remember that the rumor mill can and must be managed.

Source: Prepared by the authors.

FIGURE 4

Ten Critical Factors for Millennials

Critical Factors for Millennials	
1. *Flexibility and independence:* Freedom of self-management and trust in employees. Farewell to a fixed schedule of eight hours in the office.	2. *Fun work environment:* Having fun at work isn't incompatible with productivity and results.
3. *Access to the Internet and social media:* Facebook and Twitter are integral to their lives *and* their work.	4. *Short-term tasks:* To keep them focused, it's a good idea to assign tasks that can be completed in a short period of time.
5. *Perks and incentives:* Discount vouchers for the lunch room or cafeteria, etc. Because working nonstop hurts everyone.	6. *Career path:* Professional growth and development are more motivating than money.
7. *Mentors:* They seek mentors, not bosses.	8. *Good pay:* Even though money isn't their main motivation, that doesn't mean it's irrelevant.
9. *Opportunities to travel and meet people:* Millennials place a high value on learning and networking.	10. *Work-life balance:* No one should live only for their work, but with this generation it's absolutely essential to respect their personal lives.

Source: Prepared by the authors.

It's important to start by noting the importance of entrepreneurship for this generation. According to the «Global Entrepreneurship Monitor: 2015/16 Global Report», 50% of entrepreneurs worldwide are millennials. Along the same lines, the *Telefónica Global Millennial Survey: Global Results* notes that 72% of millennials believe there are good opportunities to become an entrepreneur in their country, and this is a career option they value as much as working for a large company.

An excellent academic record is more indispensable than ever, and millennials also need a series of skills to make them stand out from other candidates in an increasingly competitive environment where the demand for jobs exceeds the supply. In this generation, talent is seen as the ability to generate and apply knowledge. Many millennials are born leaders, people who rather than pursuing objectives focus on the present and on change, on creating and sharing new alternatives aimed at improving themselves and their environment. Like previous generations, millennials understand that information is power and that people hold on to it as a result. They aspire to make a mark on organizations and communities, and they take for granted that such bodies and groups need to constantly share and facilitate information. Knowledge is collective and cooperative; implicitly, they want the sharing of knowledge to be reciprocal (and don't understand traditional structures and ways of working based on the notion that hoarding information leads to success). Some engage in this sharing process naturally because they understand that in the global context knowledge is no longer static. And it is in this evolution—based on cooperation rather than rebellion, on respect and curiosity rather than status or convenience—that they find the life they want to lead.

For all these reasons, they need to find a company that offers exactly what they're looking for, to perceive that every company has a «soul,» that they're living organizations with different styles, values and cultures. These are the factors that determine the choices millennials make about where to work. It should be noted that members of this generation are demanding when it comes to the products they buy. It is therefore likely that they will seek to corroborate (directly, through people) any information they receive, taking advantage of the information sources available to them through their network. If a company's purported culture isn't consistently reflected in the reality of its employees' experience, millennials will quickly detect this discrepancy.

To carry out selection and recruitment policies that are effective with millennials, HR directors should focus on dynamic, cross-cutting positions that require learning and interaction with different teams and that involve the use of new technologies. Junior millennials want to do things and work with interesting people, to learn and contribute, to try things out and arrive home with things to think about and tell others about.

They want to be connected with professionals in their company and learn from people in practically all divisions, not to feel limited to a single department; to understand, and for people to know them. That's their nature. They seek to make new contacts in order to nourish and gradually expand their network. This comes naturally to people in this age bracket and is a strength that should be exploited, because the external contacts employees can reach out to are undoubtedly an asset for the company they work for. Within the framework of their cross-cutting activity it's important to ensure that junior millennials interact with people of other ages as this will be an enriching experience that helps them mature.

Given their short-term perspective, the onboarding and integration process is critical: If they're not excited about the project, the team, or the tasks they perform, they'll look for a fast way out. They also place

great importance on flexible working hours and a good work-life balance. This doesn't mean they'll bolt for the door at quitting time, but
they should, as far as possible, be able to choose when to work. They
know they're always expected to deliver value at work but don't yet
understand the rules on working hours. They're just as likely to want to
play a soccer game at 11 a.m. on a work day as to work on a report until
3 a.m. on a holiday. What matters to them is the result, not when it's
produced.

It's also advisable to create a relaxed working environment. When
working with teams of highly capable, trusted individuals, well-being
increases and people perform much better in this kind of setting. Junior millennials know this from experience and can't comprehend why a
company would accept any other kind of environment. They don't understand why many of their friends are out of work and lack opportunities,
or why there are team leaders or members who don't get excited about
the projects they're working on, who keep key information to themselves
(and undermine the team by doing so), or who think they need to deni-
grate others to advance their own interests. As a result, they're more likely to report or remark on such issues.

Tasks performed within the framework of short-term projects keep
them motivated and hold their attention more than those that require a
focused effort over a longer period. Every picture, comment or quip they
post on social media is immediately recognized with likes[3] from their followers. The workplace is no different for them: They need to be constantly evaluated and promoted, to receive frequent recognition for their work
internally and be able to publicly take pride in their accomplishments on
social media. Rather than seeing this as a problem, companies should
consider it an opportunity in terms of marketing and publicity: When it
comes to attracting new talent, nothing's more effective than the image of
a happy employee.

If they've received internal and external recognition, members of
this generation are unlikely to seek a better-paying position with another
company, provided, of course, that their salaries aren't so low as to make
them feel undervalued.

Given that millennials seek mobility—both physical and in terms of
the tasks they perform—such incentives could be seen as part of what
they get in return for their labor. Other «extras» that are in line with the

---

3. On social media, «likes» are the means by which followers show their approval
of public posts.

image the company wants to convey (e.g. discounts at stores and restaurants, on travel, etc.) are also likely to be well received. Perks are thus an increasingly important part of the overall package.

Also, if they don't find the information communicated to them within the company engaging, they won't pay attention to it. Technological tools should be used to ensure that messages are aesthetically appealing.

Finally, it's important to note the key role of communication in leading junior millennials. Managers should stay up-to-date and their attitude should be: «I don't do the kind of things you do: I don't spend my time on social media or watching videos on YouTube. Neither do I share details about my life as openly and unreservedly as you do. But I understand your concerns and can discuss them.»

A New Way to Manage People

Based on the points made in the preceding sections, we will now offer a series of specific guidelines for action that are suited to the new generation in the workforce, which by 2025 will account for 75% of employed workers.[4]

Development and Learning

Junior millennials are more concerned than the previous generation about managing their careers and professional development opportunities in the short and long term, so they can't afford to improvise. When a company hires a junior millennial, it needs to make a different kind of commitment than in the case of previous generations, and it's important to know how to handle this right.

Managers should help their millennial employees identify opportunities to put new skills into practice. This can be done by assigning them to different projects and/or temporary positions and inviting them to participate in challenging tasks, which they will always find stimulating.

It's important to study, design and communicate career plans that are realistic rather than idealized; it's better to take a conservative approach than to generate expectations so high they can't possibly be met.

---

4. Michael Page. «Millennials: Friend or foe?» http://www.michaelpage.ch/employer-centre/attraction-and-recruitment-advice/millennials-friend-or-foe, accessed April 2016.

The learning contract must be clear (based on a 70:20:10 model[5]). It should focus on the real skills the position will allow the employee to develop and how it will enhance their employability, both within the company and elsewhere. Their effort should make sense now, not only in the long term. One way to achieve this is to include international experiences as part of what goes with the job: Geographical mobility is one of the perks millennials value most highly. Moreover, fewer and fewer of them have the kind of commitments or family responsibilities that can stand in the way of this kind of mobility. Many have lived or studied in different countries and speak several languages, and they feel the world is within their grasp.

Fostering Work-Life Balance

The current trend seems to point to a progressive reduction in the physical presence of employees in the workplace. What distinguishes one individual from another will be the value they deliver, not the number of hours they put in. Increasingly, especially in high-level positions, tasks are limited to information processing, review processes and decision-making. In many cases these duties can be performed outside the office, and millennials know this perfectly well.

Millennials will keep a close eye on how managers handle their schedules and family responsibilities. Far from being admired, workaholic leaders may contribute to driving these employees away from the organization if they see that the kind of life they can expect after being promoted isn't what they want. Traditional approaches to work thus disincentivize millennials from assuming a leadership role.

One of the first measures taken should be to review company policy on IT and/or mobile devices (Internet access, laptops, smartphones, etc.) with the aim of facilitating flexible working or telework.

Adapting the Role of Status

As well as being realistic, career plans should be clearly communicated and based on diverse experiences rather than a narrow focus

5. The 70:20:10 Model for Learning and Development, based on research conducted by Michael M. Lombardo and Robert W. Eichinger, holds that individuals progress by spending 70% of their time on job-related experiences, 20% observing their environment, and 10% on courses or reading.

on promotion to a higher position in the company hierarchy («vertical growth»). This means rethinking existing perks linked to status (company cars, offices, company phones, etc.) and adapting them to the real needs of employees, who should be able to personalize their compensation—whether in the form of pay or perks—to the extent possible.

The physical layout of the workplace should be reviewed and adapted to the culture the company wants to foster. Millennials expect open spaces that promote cooperation between teams, with few physical barriers to communication. Companies should review their policy on offices, boardrooms and the design of common areas with these preferences in mind.

Middle managers must be prepared to establish the legitimacy of their leadership based on their day-to-day behavior and real expertise. Their position or power within the company may give them sufficient authority to manage people for some time, but what counts in the long run is their professional standing and the intentions revealed by their actions. As we've already mentioned, authority and hierarchies aren't automatically respected; respect must be earned.

The Limitations of Compensation As a Motivator

It's important to provide transparent information on compensation policies that's straightforward and accurately reflects current company practices, which employees should be made aware of. These policies shouldn't be opaque or arbitrary. Junior millennials want to know the rules of the game in advance. In today's workplace, middle managers have to be able to explain and defend compensation policies.

Money matters less to millennials than to members of previous generations.

More Frequent Turnover

Retention plans should provide for frequent conversations that focus on employees' careers (once a year isn't enough) with the goal of anticipating eventualities rather than avoiding them. It's also important to give millennials a sense of the significance of their activities in particular and, more broadly, of those pursued by the company. This means having a powerful mission that goes beyond the bottom line. Members of this generation want to feel that what they do is worthwhile and can make a difference; seeking to retain employees purely by economic means will prove increasingly ineffective.

Millennials are more autonomous than other generations when it comes to decision-making. As they do their jobs today, they're already thinking about their next position, and there's a limit to how long they'll wait to achieve their goals. The main reasons they decide to move on are a lack of clear purpose in their activity, difficulty achieving a good work-life balance, a bad relationship with their boss, a feeling that they're not developing within the company, and low pay.

When a millennial leaves the company, the head of the relevant division should carry out a proper exit interview; just emailing them a form to fill in isn't enough. It's vital to understand what went wrong.

Desire to Lead

While members of previous generations tend to be drawn to leadership roles by a desire to manage people and develop a team, the factors that drive junior millennials are more about themselves. The size of the team matters less to them, but they want a position where they really have the power to take action and can have an impact.

In that sense, Open XCO could be an easy and healthy praxis to invite junior employees with strong potential to participate in some management committees or other events together with senior managers in order to foster a certain degree of porosity within the organization. If well designed and executed, the impact of such practices on motivation would be hard to match. Millennials value an invitation to an event of this kind more than a promotion or salary increase. Informal breakfasts or lunches (in small groups or one-to-one) can also be very effective. The key is to do everything possible to foster intergenerational dialogue and ensure that senior leaders are aware of the talent in the pipeline.

Need for Approachable Leaders

Annual assessments provide relevant quantitative information, but it's possible to get much better results by focusing on the quantity and quality of face-to-face conversations. To be digital is to engage in a dialogue. In this context, the 9-box matrix (used to evaluate talent based on performance and potential) is a tool that offers transparency. Ideally, it should be used at all levels.

Leaders must be able to offer employees a realistic prospect of career advancement in the short term, and middle managers should be given the tools and knowledge they need to manage these critical, and sometimes complicated, conversations. As we've already indicated, employees should be provided with frequent feedback that has a positive focus and is based on their strengths, which are the tools they can use to bring more value to the company.

Developing an Attractive Culture

The corporate activities used to engage millennials should be fun, audacious, simple, and not too formal. There are countless ways to generate a sense of engagement. For a millennial, their birthday is a really important event that should practically be a national holiday, so one very simple option is to give them the big day off (or at least half a day).

Onboarding has become a critical process, so nothing should be left to chance. The induction process is a unique opportunity to generate emotional bonds with new hires while also motivating those who have been with the organization for some time. It must be well executed, friendly, and include someone who the new millennial employees can identify with, who will be available to them during their first weeks on the job, and who can facilitate their social integration. Their first day should be a memorable one.

If the onboarding process (which starts with the job offer process and ends six months after the new employee's start date) cannot be completely redesigned, at the very least, steps should be taken to ensure that hygiene factors are properly addressed. This starts with making sure each new employee is welcomed by someone on the first day and shown their desk and computer.

It's important to ensure that climate and opinion surveys cover onboarding in order to get feedback on this process and on how new employees perceive the organizational culture in general. An effort should also be made to humanize the tone of corporate communications and those coming from the management committee. This means using language that's accessible and sometimes even informal. Bear in mind that many members of this generation would rather be unemployed than work in a job they hate.

Recognition

Promoting a culture of recognition requires the genuine involvement of the management committee and company leaders, which should be made evident every day: formally, through corporate events, and informally, by means of conversations and off-the-cuff remarks. While the need for recognition is common to all generations, for millennials it's almost as important to be recognized by their peers as by their superiors. It's therefore a good idea to develop tactical reward programs, which most commonly involve monetary rewards. Recompense may come in the form of small bonuses, lunches or dinners out, coaching sessions, extra vacation days, and so on.

The approach to performance management needs to be reconsidered. Managers should ask whether performance measures distinguish sufficiently between employees, and whether the system in place serves to identify the best performers and reward them accordingly. This generation wants to stand out and compete.

Sharing the Good and the Bad

It may prove useful to involve millennials in employer branding activities. This would entail appointing and training them as social media brand ambassadors, taking them to job fairs, involving them in the recruitment of recent graduates, and so on. An effort should be made to identify employees who are social leaders by monitoring their activity on social media, and it's important to ensure that anyone chosen to represent the firm on social media is going to work in its interest in this context.

Millennials can play a valuable role in internal focus groups aimed at understanding matters such as their perception of the company's strengths, the employer's role, and the differential aspects of the strategy for recruiting new employees and attracting talent.

Another effective approach may be a special promotion policy for new employees—an integration stage (lasting two years, for instance) during which promotions are more frequent (every six months) and each step forward is linked to the acquisition of clearly defined knowledge or experience. These promotions need not be linked to pay rises, but this predefined process should be streamlined and fast-paced, and it should ensure frequent recognition of new hires. This means rethinking promotion, which instead of involving advancement through a hierarchy should entail a progressive increase in the scope of a position and the responsibility that goes with it.

Digital Natives

Companies should introduce reverse mentoring so millennials can assist members of other generations by sharing their knowledge and experience of new technologies and social media. As far as possible, younger employees can also advise on and oversee related tasks in all areas of the business.

They can also be asked to participate in the critical examination and analysis of technology so they can give feedback on new purchases or developments in this area. Millennials, who have grown up in constant contact with technological devices, can often provide valuable input on what might work (or fail to) in real life. Another area where they can play a useful role is in testing corporate social media strategy.

How They See Their Leaders

In 2015, the IESE surveyed 22,000 managers from around the world, 85% of whom were born after 1985. The questions focused on the leadership style of their bosses, and the results offer a clear and positive road map to chart a course through the «concrete and glass jungle» that must be traversed when taking up and settling into a new position. The key conclusion is that people should be led based on the what they are, not what they should be.

The respondents said two thirds of their bosses were reactive when it came to tackling changes and that this was due mainly to fear of failure, reluctance to move out of their comfort zone, lack of perspective, and the rigidity of their approaches. The message is clear: Leaders should anticipate events—with caution and sound judgment—in order to control how they develop rather than being controlled by them. And the reason is obvious: People expect their leaders to address challenges in a timely manner. These results also suggest that the respondents in turn are likely to be more reactive than proactive, and that companies should therefore take steps to help them act boldly as well as competently.

There's no substitute for trust in a leader. The respondents think that in order to trust their bosses more, they need them to be more self-critical and transparent and to take decisions. They also believe that their bosses tend to be overly ambitious and optimistic. Too much emphasis is placed on what superiors should do, when half the time it would be enough for them to know what they should *not* do. At the same time, the deficiencies people identify in their bosses probably point to qualities the observers themselves lack. Much of the pervasive uncertainty we experience is because the reasons we have for trusting each other are few and not particularly strong. Without moral minimums (which as things stand are maximums) life in society becomes unbearable.

The respondents also believe their bosses would get more out of them if they told them more about what they want and why, encouraged teamwork, and helped them improve (through coaching). We know organizations aren't more effective because they have better people. In fact, it's just the opposite: If they have better people, it's because they encourage them to develop by creating a favorable environment through the example set by bosses and the habits (skills) inculcated by company policy. Habits—if they're positive we call them «virtues,» and if negative, «vices»—give concrete expression to a company's values (positive or negative) by applying them to its day-to-day activity through decision-making. If bosses suffer from «moral anorexia,» subordinates are bound to fall victim to the same condition sooner rather than later.

When asked to identify what they saw as the main skills that led to good results, there was broad agreement that the key factors were customer orientation, business vision, and effective resource management. The higher a leader is in the organizational chart, the more tempted they will be to focus on what's happening inside the company, which keeps them from seeing the bigger picture. Unless the leader makes an extraordinary effort, they will not see what's happening outside the firm, where results are reflected. The reality of the market is beyond the control of any company. The processes involved in a new manager taking charge can be managed to a large extent, but they cannot be completely controlled.

Finally, the respondents firmly believe there are too many charismatic and visionary leaders—it was about time!—and that we need more who are approachable, entrepreneurial, and strategic in their thinking. However, charisma still pays dividends because subordinates are as likely to be seduced by this quality as to complain of its undesired effects.

The role of bosses is to eliminate our excuses for being mediocre by pushing us and helping us grow as they also develop, without forgetting a crucial fact: The only person anyone truly has direct control over is him or herself.

* * *

As has happened time and again, younger millennials will be enriched by contact with their older peers and members of previous generations, and this interaction will enable them to develop their full potential, both in the professional domain and at a personal level. They already have great skills, but not all the needed maturity to make them perform in collective environments, such companies. Management policies must be adaptable to how they are, in addition to enhancing their capabilities. In turn, companies can improve their proactivity and effectiveness by learning from them and be at their height, however small.

EXHIBIT

Exhibit 1
Professional Aspirations of University and Executive MBA Students

University Students: Professional Aspirations

1. To give the best of myself and be promoted within the company; to have a job that involves varied work, that I find fulfilling, and that allows me to have a positive impact on the community.

2. To attain my professional ideal in a job with values and an international dimension, where good work is respected and I feel fulfilled, happy, and well paid enough to live comfortably.

3. Very high, but always keep my feet on the ground, without being at the top, but creating my own top in something I enjoy doing.

4. To get established in a company and continually develop as a professional, reaching a position of high responsibility and importance that allows me to be one of the select group of professionals who focus on the common good, and, in so doing, to provide help to those who need it.

5. Right now my personal and professional aspirations are the same: to become a great professional, someone who's respected and has significant responsibility, and to do a job that excites me and generates values which contribute to social development.

6. After completing further training in a graduate program, to set up my own company so I can work in something I enjoy and have decision-making power (I want to be autonomous).

7. To become a competent professional and a good leader, to get to the top with honor and decency, and to have responsibilities that are significant but allow me to maintain a good work-life balance.

8. In the short term, to get a very good job, but in the long term, to have one that's compatible with my personal life, makes the hours I spend at work meaningful, and allows me to learn something new every day.

9. Not to be slaughtered like a lamb.

Executive MBA Students: Professional Aspirations

1. To set up my own company or pursue new initiatives within the family business, and to hire some people at risk of social exclusion.

2. To be happy in my work and become a good boss who makes a difference and gets things done by setting an example rather than just making demands, and to be respected for that.

3. Not to fear failure, and to be brave and honest in my decisions in order to achieve my goals.

4. To develop in a job that makes me feel fulfilled and provides me (and my team) with a good salary so I can start a family.

5. To give my labor to organizations whose values are aligned with my own and to customers. To achieve more of a leadership role and more responsibility so I can take decisions that have an impact on society and on company strategy.

6. To lead a medium-sized team made up of eight to twenty people who are motivated to meet challenges that go beyond those companies generally pursue, and for our achievements to be appreciated by the rest of the organization.

7. To be a good professional who's highly recognized within my company for my orientation towards internal customers, my contribution to the firm's performance, and my proactive approach to serving others (bosses, my team, customers, etc.).

8. To improve every day, have fun at work, and reach a point where I'm working on things that really matter: «Choose a job you love and you'll never have to work a day in your life» (Confucius).

9. To continue to work and grow in my sector; to be part of a company that's driven to innovate and that takes care of its customers; and, in addition to growing professionally, to work hard so I can lead a team; to enjoy my work and care about the product or project I'm working on.

10. To hold a position as general manager or on the senior management team of a multinational company (in my company, 600 of a total of 152,000 employees hold positions at this level).

11. To earn the opportunity to retire before I turn 40.

Part Two

The three real cases described below aim to illustrate current situations of companies in which existing generations converge in the labor market; embodied in unique people with their vital priorities, styles and behaviors; where the youngest members play a stellar role, both because of the presence they deploy and because of the impact of their actions.

The reading of the cases yields its best fruit when the reader asks, while his eyes run from line to line, what he would do if he were one of the protagonists. Actions are usually preceded by a decision, better or worse founded. It is the reader's responsibility to immerse himself in reality and interpret the data with their intelligence and emotions.

The case of Microsoft offers the opportunity to explore how people from different generational origins converge and diverge, and what everyone from the top of direction of companies to the company managers face in order to manage expectations and realities.

The Salesforce case allows us to track the youngest members' adaptation to new company which, in reality, involves a new culture, built on shared values and operational behavior. It also allows us to delve into what concerns us as human beings.

The case of American Valley invites us to explore the meaning of the management programs of young professionals with high performance potential and the effect it has on the organization, both in its positive and negative aspects

The examination of a case becomes an exciting adventure because of the learning experience that can be extracted from it; it only requires a proactive attitude, the same as millennials demand of those of us who are not millennials.

Chapter 7
The Leadership of Millennials at Microsoft

Rocío Is Leaving

«Hi, Luisa. Rocío[1] is leaving. There doesn't seem to be any going back. She didn't want to tell me why, but it's bad news that I wasn't expecting,» said Ana, director of the Major Accounts and Partners Unit at Microsoft Ibérica, to Luisa, the Human Resources director.

«No way. She's one of our best MACH members. I'm going to talk to her immediate supervisor and decide what to do,» Luisa answered, worried.

Luisa had been the HR manager at Microsoft Ibérica for barely six months. Rocío was one of the people Microsoft was counting on to develop the company's immediate future. She was 26 years old, a telecommunications engineer and a member of the MACH program, the Microsoft Academy for College Hires, which included 17 other promising young millennials.[2] She had just returned from a two-week training course in the Redmond headquarters, which was regarded as a real honor at Microsoft.

After confirming that Rocío's business partner in the HR Department was also surprised and dismayed by the news, Luisa called Manuel, the head of the department where Rocío worked.

---

1. Some names have been changed for the sake of confidentiality.
2. The generation born between 1985 and 1999.

«Hi, Manuel. I just found out that Rocío has decided to leave. Did you know anything about this?» Luisa said.

«Ana just told me and it caught me as off-guard as it did you. Actually nobody in the department knew anything, but I think if we talk to her we may still be able to keep her. Give me some time and I'll call you back with her reaction,» Manuel said.

Twenty minutes later, the telephone in Luisa's office rang again.

«There's nothing we can do. I really don't get it. In January, I nominated her to go to the training in Redmond because I had full confidence in her. She is one of our best, as you know through the people review committees.»[3]

When she hung up the phone, Luisa pondered: How could it be that a person with such positive ratings by the company, whose salary was considerably higher than the market, would decide to leave? («Could it be that the Human Resources policies are poorly gauged?») And what bothered her even more: «Is it contagious?» Luisa loved managing and interacting with the youngest and most valuable members of the company, and she was keenly interested in understanding how they had lost one of the most talented members of the team, even if this meant changing her day's schedule.

Luisa Izquierdo

Luisa Izquierdo started studying for her bachelor's degree in Law in 1992, and one year later she added another major in Psychology. After earning both degrees, she got a master's in HR – Compensation and Benefits. She did an internship at the Human Resources Department of Carrefour and worked in consulting for one year (at Norconsult). After spending two years at Amena, in 2001 she began her career at Honeywell, an American multinational in the industrial sector, where she grew professionally. In October 2015, after spending 14 years in different managerial positions within the Human Resources departments of different businesses within the company, and with responsibility over different countries, Luisa was hired by Microsoft Ibérica. She truly enjoyed her work and had always seen her role as essential and totally strategic within the company.

---

3. People review committees were specific management committees which regularly engaged in in-depth monitoring of the young hires with the most potential.

The project that Microsoft put her in charge of was one of the main reasons she decided to leave Honeywell. The challenge of managing the HR Department in Spain of a large, global technology company and the associated career plan were also essential factors in her decision. After more than 10 years in international positions in which Luisa had traveled 80% of the time, she was eager to return to figure out the local market and spend more time at home.

As a member of the management committee, she had to meet for a people review every three months. At these meetings, which lasted an entire day, the individual needs of each person at Microsoft were reviewed and the organization's talent was analyzed exhaustively.

Just like the rest of the senior management team, she was required to be a person who expressed herself clearly, generated positive energy, and delivered results. Her performance was reviewed each year according to the impact it had on the business and her capacity to work with her colleagues.

Microsoft

Founded on April 4, 1975, by Bill Gates and Paul Allen, Microsoft was a multinational devoted to computer technology with the mission of developing, manufacturing, licensing, and supporting a wide range of hardware and software products for IT devices. In 2016, the company generated an income of around $85.32 billion (see **Exhibit 1**).

Microsoft claimed that it sought to reinvent productivity to help each person and each organization do more and achieve more. The strategy depended on three main cornerstones: people, culture and customers. Regarding the people in the organization, the company actively sought to achieve high levels of diversity in its workforce and leaders, in addition to attracting the best and the brightest. To do so, its human resources policies revolved around hiring and developing the best leaders, recognizing and encouraging women with technical skills, promoting the study of computer science at universities, encouraging women to study computer science, fostering student diversity, hiring the best and the brightest and celebrating what technology can do to train people. Microsoft promoted a culture of inclusion through training in cultural competencies and strategies to manage diversity, while also offering flexible schedules and programs to help employees reach a better balance between their professional and personal lives.

In terms of its customers, the company made an effort to offer technological innovation through devices and services which could inspire people of all ages and skills, as well as by eliminating barriers, improving lives and strengthening communities.

The high competitiveness in the Microsoft environment (see **Exhibit 2**) was primarily characterized by the changes taking place in this environment, which required employees to be wary of new threats at all times and to use learning as a way to deal with them. The stress and pressure that this situation placed on employees led to a mental overload that the company wanted to avoid. This is why they were given workshops on healthy eating and habits.

In an interview with one of the leading radio stations in the country, Pilar López, the country manager for Spain, had acknowledged,

> «Microsoft is a company that is the midst of transformation. From being the company of Windows, Office and Word, it has also become the company of the cloud, of cloud technology and productivity, and it has become a company that allows people to access technology in a more natural way, using products like Minecraft or virtual or augmented reality. This transformation process required different people, not only in terms of the home but also in business.»

Microsoft Ibérica

In 2016, the Madrid subsidiary's results surpassed $12 million, with income of over $180 million (see **Exhibit 3**). The staff included slightly more than 700 employees, 35% of whom were women, a fantastic figure for a tech company, which reflected the efforts made in recent years to attract more diverse staff (see **Exhibit 4**). The figure was even higher on the management committee, which was 44% female (see **Exhibit 5**).

In the interview mentioned above, López stated,

> «My career has been defined by teams with very few women, and this is something that we have to change. Microsoft is a company that has been working towards gender equality for a long time, and in a sector with very few women (less than 20%), we have gotten our company to almost double this amount, so almost half the members of the management committee that I lead are women. This fosters normalcy and the fact that work climates are more pleasant, constructive, and similar to those of our customers and to real life.»

Microsoft's concern with creating a work environment where employees felt like members of a community was embodied by a 2013 change of policies that encouraged collaboration. With this change, the program for talented young workers, which had been underway since

2005 truly came to the fore. Luisa explained the importance of this new collaborative culture and the way to achieve it:

«Through small gestures, like the availability of collaborative spaces. In our case, the offices are designed to be environments of exchange where you can go if you have something to do with others. It is important to create open, spacious areas which foster innovation thanks to cloud information, which allows you to collaborate with others no matter where you and they are and to send a really consistent message. In our organization, we say that collaboration is an essential asset, and we even recognize it as such in tools like performance review, in which it is one of the factors that is measured and rewarded.»

All the employees, but especially the young ones, were asked to bring passion, a desire to learn, and generosity about sharing their knowledge. The HR Department regarded employee flexibility as essential. What is more, it was hard for them to work with people with pre-established ideas. Furthermore, the company's policies for those who wanted to remain with the company but change departments or activities were clear. «If someone with talent wanted to stay in the company, it had mechanisms that could help them along in their professional development,» Luisa said.

The MACH Program

Every year since 2005, Microsoft had been investing in 15 or 16 recent graduates to train them in a program designed to build the company's next generation of talent. The new hires had to have the ability to learn, a passion for technology and innovation and the ability to work with others and on teams. They also were asked to have had different experiences through which they could bring diversity to the company. The goal of the program was met, since 83% of those who had participated in it were still working within different areas of Microsoft (see **Exhibit 6**).

Luisa mentioned, regarding new hires and the company's policy regarding them

«I like their passion, their curiosity, their capacity for commitment and their critical, nonconformist spirit. Generally speaking, we don't like arrogance, a lack of flexibility, and the inability to put yourself in others' shoes.»

The MACH experience consisted of in-person and virtual human resources training with the global MACH team, which allowed its members to connect with the MACH community and with local Human Resources directors, as well as allowing their managers to keep up with their development and training.

During their first few months with Microsoft, the MACH participants attended an onboarding program, where they received training on how to integrate into the company. After that, they held a real position in the company and performed the jobs of that position. At the beginning of the second year, they took a seven-day training course geared towards increasing their impact in Microsoft. Meanwhile, during the two years of the program, they received virtual sessions focused on their specific professional needs (see **Exhibit 7**).

The program's intention was to hire the talent with the most potential in the market and to develop those employees so that they could be promoted more quickly than usual. To do this, MACH participants also received three training sessions per year at the company's most important headquarters. The cross-cutting nature of the projects allowed them to gain better visibility and monitoring, and Luisa met with them once a month to give them a picture of the status of both the company and the sector.

The participants in this program began with a score of 58,[4] with the intention that they could quickly reach 61 upon completing the two-year program. A score of 62 was needed to land a managerial position, and 67 to reach the management committee. Pilar López had a score of 69. The ascent in each of these levels came with higher compensation, but the specific amount was determined in individual negotiations between each employee and the Human Resources Department, as well as by the characteristics of the job and their own compensation at the time of the promotion.

Having gone through the MACH program was still a distinction within the company, so at the end of the two years promotions were expected to come more quickly than the organization's average. However, going through this program was not considered a prerequisite, and sometimes employees who had not participated in it were promoted more quickly.

The program participants' compensation was similar to that of other company employees and consisted of a fixed amount and a variable amount which ranged from 20% to 50% of the end salary, depending on the position. Stock options and training programs were also an important

---

4. Microsoft structures the organization through a system of levels and points which determine compensation.

part of employees' salaries. At Microsoft, the goal was for compensation packages to not be merely economic.

«Innovation in compensation goes beyond offering employees a value proposition focused only on remuneration. In addition to offering a competitive salary, a short- and long-term incentive program that rewards performance and identification with the company's values, and a package of perks that shows employees that we care about them and their families, we should also add other elements into the mix to make your company an attractive place that retains talent: an interesting package which excites them, an atmosphere in which professionals feel that they can develop both personally and professionally, a flexible environment that allows them to integrate their personal and work lives.»

Diversity was a key point in a group of employees who were asked to be innovative and share a customer-centered approach, intercultural experience, ambition and energy.

«Gorka, I've finally solved the puzzle. Let's go get some drinks and leave the new challenges for Monday,» Álvaro said with a smile that concealed his satisfaction with a job well done.

«Great, let the others know while I finish sending these emails,» Gorka said.

«The ones with the reports, right?» Álvaro said.

«Yeah, I hate this part but I'm almost done,» Gorka said.

It was 7 p.m. on a Friday, and Gorka, Álvaro, Israel, and Virginia, the liveliest of the MACH group at Microsoft, were meeting to end the week with beer at a bar near La Finca, on the outskirts of Madrid, where the company's Spain offices were located. They didn't usually finish so late on Fridays, but that week had been exhausting, as work meetings had been piled on top of preparations for two social projects, and the Spartan Race was drawing near, so they had to be prepared.

The most serious and traditional of them all was Gorka. His technical depth along with his social and sales skills, which he displayed at events, had given Pilar López, the country manager, the chance to know about him. Álvaro was well-liked by his colleagues and superiors for his dedication to one of the company's star projects. His willingness to catch the high-speed train any day at any time and travel to manage the project was one of his hallmarks. Israel was the most outgoing of all the MACHs in his group, and he was best at enjoying and furthering many after-work projects. Finally, Virginia was probably the smartest of the group. Her personality and constant desire to learn led her to earn a name for herself within the company.

The Hiring Process

«Wow, what a week! Do you remember when you started? I feel like the difficulty of the interview process and all the tests they put us through were actually just a reflection of reality,» Virginia said. After graduating with a degree in Telecommunications from the Polytechnic, she had begun the GAIA Program with an internship at Telefónica.

«You're right. Yours was the same as mine, right? First an online questionnaire to see how we would act in different situations, then we had to record a video answering pretty much the same questions, then a Skype interview with the HR Department in London, and finally a six-hour appointment at the assessment center with two presentations and a business case study. I remember it was fun, but at some point I thought the process would never end,» Gorka said.

«That's true. They changed it your year. I got out of doing the interview with London,» said Álvaro, still happy with his performance.

«I was already inside doing an internship, so I had an interview with HR, another with the manager, and another with the hiring manager, with whom I worked every day, and the assessment center,» Israel said.

The Appeal of Microsoft

«So what brought you to Microsoft? Did you have any other job offers?» Gorka asked as he put his beer on the table.

«I had offers from major consulting firms, but that wasn't my scene. I have friends who are holed up from eight in the morning to nine at night; it's not like we don't work long hours, but here the work is different and more dynamic. You work better and learn more,» Virginia said. «Microsoft was a large company where you could develop a career in the middle term and perhaps even in the long term.»

«You're right. I didn't consider working for the 'assembly lines' either. Here I was going to get international experiences and be near innovation. It was a chance I couldn't pass up,» Álvaro said.

«My case was a bit different. Even before I started college, I had been in an innovation club at the Polytechnic led by Microsoft. That gave me the chance to gain visibility and get to know the company. I saw that I could have career prospects here and make my mark on something great. That encouraged me to make the decision to join the company,» Gorka said.

Expectations vs. Reality

«I don't know if this happened to you, but I remember that when I joined Microsoft I thought I would be in the big leagues, and I quickly realized that I had colleagues who probably hadn't even made it to the minors because of their attitude and performance. Did anything like this happen to you?» Gorka asked.

«Not exactly, but I do see that responsibilities pile up more quickly than the rank, which grows more slowly than the expectations I had been led to understand. Plus, we have the same responsibilities as other people with salaries four or five times higher than ours, and we often get more done than they do,» Israel said.

«It's true that it kind of seems like unfair treatment, but they've been at the company ten years more than we have. It'll come,» Virginia said.

«Don't forget – we're the next Satya![5] Or don't you pay attention in the international training programs?» Israel said jokingly.

«Those programs are great. I love the trips and the possibility of being near the bigwigs in the company, but I think they should cut back a bit on the American dream messaging. More than one person has gotten such high hopes that when they're back here they've lost motivation and taken the exit ramp. Have you guys ever considered it?» Álvaro said.

«Wait what? You mean you want to leave us?» Virginia asked, knowing that for the time being Álvaro had no intentions of jumping ship.

«No, not at all. You know I like it here, but some things just don't make sense. Marcos left last year, and now he's come back with the same responsibilities and twice the salary. That doesn't sound like a bad strategy to me. Plus, today I've gotten another call from a headhunter asking me how I'm doing,» Álvaro said.

«If you've got big news on your future, I'm going to order another round so we can toast to it,» Gorka said.

«No, not at all. I don't have any news yet, I was just thinking out loud. I'm all in at Microsoft until death, but I want them to be all in with us, too. Anyway, go ahead and order that round. This terrace is great,» Álvaro said.

Getting calls from headhunters with tempting offers to leave Microsoft and embark upon a new adventure at another company was something that happened more often than Luisa would have liked. Approximately each week, some member of the MACH program got a call. Luisa was used to meeting with MACH members who wanted to leave or had offers from companies like Tesla, whose projects tended to be appealing,

5. CEO of Microsoft.

or Salesforce, where the salary and training policy was very aggressive, or startups that offered enticing opportunities and projects.

When the motive was purely economic, something could be arranged if the employee was upfront about it and wanted to stay at the company without feeling demotivated because they had let the opportunity slip by. When the offer consisted of a more attractive project, Luisa understood the situation and tried to leave the door open for them to return in the future. «The way you're talking about it, I'm really happy that you have this opportunity. When you get tired of it, before going somewhere else, call us to see where we are,» she remembered having told a former employee, as she tried to discern the causes that led Rocío to decide to leave.

Luisa had seen that the new generations of Microsoft employees were not proactive in looking outside the company as long as it was capable of seeing and understanding their concerns. Plus, she had also noticed that MACH participants who had been doing the same job for six or eight months were more likely to leave the company. This is why she felt a greater obligation to get to know them better in order to properly manage and motivate them.

Mentors: The Importance of People Management

«Well, I do have some good news for you,» said Israel. His announcement brought looks of expectation to his colleagues' faces. «The other day on my trip to the London headquarters, I sat down to talk with a senior manager from there. It turns out that he was Israeli and liked my name. I think that that's why he agreed to be my mentor, so now I have a new mentor in Europe,» he said.

«Your ability to attract mentors is really enviable. I mean, in your very first week here you asked Luisa for a one-on-one,» Gorka said, applauding the motivation his colleague showed to improve every day and gain visibility in the company.

«If I change my name to India, maybe Satya will like it and take me to the US to be his right-hand woman,» Virginia said.

The four kept up the laughter and jokes for a while. A new mentor meant a significant opportunity for learning and promotion for Israel, so everyone was happy with his news.

«So how's the new job?» Israel asked Virginia, who had changed departments just one week ago.

«Great,» Virginia said. «Actually, our chance to rotate departments is a real privilege. It's not like I wasn't happy before, but I felt like I had maxed out my potential there.»

«Something similar happened to me. After two years doing consulting work in the banking sector, I needed a change of scene. My manager saw it, too, and his help was essential. Have you guys ever had a bad manager?» Álvaro asked.

«Not bad, but I have had a few who only focused on the business. I think that it depends on the department, but for example, in Sales, to reach that position you have to be a killer and make sure the honchos know who you are. It's to be expected that they often don't have the time to worry about what's happening below them,» Gorka said.

«That's true. They have to meet their own sales targets. They rarely have the time to worry about us. Still, I think that the higher the position in the company, the more interested they are in listening to you. In London, everyone had a minute to sit down and talk, and they all wanted to know what our dealings with customers were like,» Israel recounted, remembering his trip. «Have you guys ever used the platform to blow the whistle on a problem with your managers?» he asked.

«No way! Actually, I don't know anyone who has used it. I don't even think it works. They must go to a nebula filled with cobwebs which no one ever visits,» Gorka said jokingly.

They continued to laugh and make jokes about it. There was a great feeling among the four. They worked long hours together and shared many interests outside of work. They already knew each other well and this made their conversations relaxed and filled with laughter.

The Passage of Time: Different Generations

«I remember that when I joined Microsoft, I would stick my nose in everything. I still want to learn and grow, to have initiatives and give 200%, but now I find that I'm beginning to reject jobs that I would have accepted before,» Virginia said.

«I'm doing the exact same thing,» Álvaro said conspiratorially. «When I came here, I said yes to everything and I offered to help wherever I could. Now I'm more discerning. I think that experience has taught me to know who is offering me a project that will sink in the middle of the ocean after hours and hours, and which projects may be completed successfully. I think that all of us who join this program are like that; we like to be involved in everything, and that's why they hire us,» he said.

«I've changed, too,» Israel said. «Now that I've got a family, I'm beginning to shift roles, thinking about my personal future and having enough time for it. Would you change anything about what we do at Microsoft?» he asked.

«I'm fine,» Álvaro replied quickly. «I came from having spent two years chained to my desk at a consulting firm, so the flexibility and freedom we have to work here is amazing.»

«Álvaro, you're like the perfect embodiment of this company's DNA. I'm sure if you spend two or three years in Redmond, you'll be here till you die,» Israel said.

«I'd change the reporting structure,» Virginia said. «We have to answer to so many people and I just want to do my job.»

«That's true. I call meetings that last less than an hour and people look at me like I'm a weirdo. I think that they're really bad at managing their calendars,» Israel said.

Generational Differences

«What I'd like to learn from my bosses is what they know and their own experiences, although sometimes it's a letdown,» Virginia said.

«I think that our generation and the ones after us are soft and getting softer (maybe there are more temper tantrums than there should be), and I also think that we need to be a bit more chill. Sometimes we kind of lose sight of reality and want more,» Álvaro said.

«Well, at parties they're worse. They call me 'red flag' because sometimes I have to tell them to behave properly,» Israel said.

At a conference held a few days earlier, Ana Alonso had said,

«Millennials at Microsoft are not different. For other companies they may be, and demonstrating their value is a motivation for them the we should know how to use, but when I think about my team, I don't see any barriers between the new generations of employees and the others. At Microsoft, we've grasped that they contribute a great deal to the company. Our millennials, just like the company's other employees, are dynamic, nimble, goal- and customer-oriented, resilient, and like to continue to receive training.»

The Viewpoint of Some Managers

After completing a master's in Telecommunications Engineering, Ana Alonso began her professional career at HP, where she held different jobs within the Technical Support Department. After almost eight years at the company and earning an MBA, she began to work for Sun Microsystems as a Customer Operations Manager. In 2008, she took an executive training course on leadership at a school in London, and one year later she began to work for Microsoft in its Solutions and Alliances Department. After two years as the director of Strategic Accounts, in October 2014 she was put in charge of the company's Major Accounts and Partners Department, a job she held when the events in this case happened. Her job was to lead the Microsoft team working with its customers to drive the business and turn the company into a partner in the digital transformation of all sectors. To do so, she led a team of more than 80 people.

Ana had just arrived at La Finca and was getting ready to leave for a meeting with the other managers and executives when she ran into Luisa.

«Have you been able to figure anything else out about Rocío's reasons for leaving?» Ana asked after exchanging pleasantries.

«Not much, really. Manuel thinks that we still have a chance to keep her, and I've made an appointment to speak to her tomorrow. Why do you think she's leaving?» Luisa asked.

«Few talented people have left us for money, so I don't think it's a problem that can't be solved. She's probably gotten an offer to work on another project that is more interesting to her,» Ana said.

«You're right. What do you think we should change?» Luisa asked.

«We'll have to see what we can do to retain our top talent more effectively, although we already offer plenty of project mobility,» Ana said.

«True, there's a lot of internal mobility, but like in all companies, there is a ceiling in access to the management committee. Microsoft has changed in recent years and needs to hire external talent in order to keep developing in such a dynamic sector, seeking diversity and avoiding an endogenous climate,» Luisa said. «In the past, only 5% of our new hires came from outside, and now they're up to 40%. Some people don't realize that. Perhaps our managers should better understand people's needs and the feedback they give. I think that we should have honest conversations about their professional career and about what they should work on and develop, not only with MACH participants but with all employees,» she continued.

«The good thing about Microsoft is that the market forces us to constantly change, so we have to constantly identify new responsibilities and offer them to talented employees,» Ana said.

Sergio and Raúl were headed to the same meeting as Ana and Luisa. After working together at Microsoft for over 15 years, they had become close friends and often met for breakfast. They were level 62 and 63 account managers, respectively.

«Sergio, I'm thinking about changing departments. I don't feel as motivated in Sales as I used to,» Raúl said.

«Buddy, you know that there are two Microsofts here: the headquarters, where decisions are made, and the subsidiary, where they are carried out. We work in a Sales subsidiary, so in any other department the chances of promotion are going to be relatively small,» Sergio said. «But you know what Luisa says: 'The key to reaching senior management is identifying with the company's values and mission and being capable of operating at the pace demanded by the industry.'»

«Another option is going to Europe,[6] but that's a bit complicated. I'd have the same salary with less pressure, and I'd act as a liaison between the corporation and the subsidiaries. If it works out well, I could take a leap forward in the organization, and if not, I could accept the beginning of my retirement,» Raúl said.

«That would allow you to keep working from Madrid, and maybe get back your motivation, but you know that the second possibility is more likely than the first,» Sergio said.

«I do. Since we can work from home and don't have a set location in the office, mobility wouldn't be a problem with the change. Plus, I would have better career projection there, given that in the subsidiary, from our job as individual contributors we can only be promoted to general managers or members of the management committee,» Raúl said.

«Remember that despite that, sales are in the subsidiary, so in Europe you'd be less visible,» Sergio said.

«Well, but I'd also hold periodic meetings with other subsidiaries and other headquarters in Europe,» Raúl said.

«As long as they don't continue the dynamic of holding follow-up meetings online,» Sergio said.

«Every day I'm more and more sure that we should have started out in the corporation. Careers move more quickly there since the chances of promotion are greater because there are more jobs,» Raúl said.

«You're right. There's a ceiling in the subsidiary. We moved up to management positions pretty quickly, but from there on it's pretty hard to keep getting promotions. Before they promoted in-house, and every now and then someone from the outside, but now I get the sense that you have to come from outside in order to be promoted. Can you see yourself moving to another company?» Sergio asked.

«Actually, I hadn't really considered it. Because of Microsoft's culture, there are no meetings before nine in the morning or after 6:30 at night, so I

---

6. Europe was the part of Microsoft in charge of connecting the corporate office with the subsidiary offices. Each member of the management committee in Spain had a person in Europe to whom they reported.

can take my kids to school, plus our compensation is a bit higher than the market rate. The downside is that often we have too much work for a single eight-hour day and we have to work at night,» Raúl said.

«What do you think about the younger generations? Do you think they'll get further?» Sergio asked.

«I think they're really good and really well trained. You can tell that they're full of enthusiasm and work hard at what they like, of course, but I'm not so convinced that they are capable of working hard on the less motivating daily tasks,» Raúl said.

«Here, no one has interns or secretaries, so we managers also have to do the back-office work,» Sergio said.

«I sense that they're eager to be promoted, but no one at Microsoft is promoted that quickly. They'll be the future of the company, and yet just another fish in the sea,» Raúl said.

«When you think you've got a stairway to heaven and you realize that you're missing steps, it's not surprising that they think about other professional options,» Sergio said.

«But that staircase actually does exist; look at how quickly the MACH participants are promoted in their first years here. We never had that opportunity,» Raúl said.

«True, but once they reach level 62, it's as hard for them to get promotions as it is for everyone else, and I think that they don't have the patience they need to get there. To keep getting promoted, you've got to do lots of networking and work really hard, on things that aren't as visible from above, too,» Sergio said.

«And even that won't necessarily cut it. To reach that level, they're going to take at least six to seven years. I'm not sure that their expectations are going to be met as quickly as they want,» Raúl said.

The Conversation With Rocío

«Hi, Luisa. You wanted to see me?» Rocío said.

«Yes, come on in! What terrible news! I heard you're leaving!» Luisa said. «I was so disappointed to hear it because I think you've got such a promising future in the company, and if you don't mind, I'd really like to understand why you're leaving and find out if there was anything we could have done differently to prevent it from getting to this point.»

«No, nothing at all. I've really liked it here. I love the company and my boss is great,» Rocío said.

«Hmm, then it's hard to understand why you're leaving. Let me explain: I've been with the company for six months and your name has come up in the LT.[7] I know you've been working really hard; in fact, look,» she said, opening her computer to show Rocío her screen. «I have a proposal for your promotion, which would have raised your salary, but it mainly shows that your hard work has been noticed. You've been here two and a half years, investing a great deal of effort and dedication to make a name for yourself, and you've achieved it. And now that the time has come to start reaping the benefits of your hard work, you decide to leave. It's such a pity. So tell me: have you been offered a project you can't refuse?»

«No, I'm leaving to do something fairly similar to what I'm doing here,» Rocío said.

«I don't get it, Rocío,» Luisa responded.

«Well, there was a point when I didn't feel appreciated,» Rocío said.

«That's interesting and it doesn't at all match what I've been told; Manuel even told me that he sent you to do a course in Redmond for which he had to specifically nominate you,» Luisa said.

«So that course was a personal nomination?» Rocío asked.

«Yes, Manuel had one spot for himself and he chose you.»

«I had no idea. I just got an invitation by email,» Rocío said. «Plus, the team where I am has gone from 6 to 12 members, and their integration over these months hasn't been very easy. We've had to spend hours and hours teaching the new hires how to work at Microsoft, and some of them earn more than those of us who were already here,» she continued.

«Look, Rocío, it's true that these hires aren't familiar with Microsoft, but they have ten years of experience and a lot to offer the company. They're at a more advanced point in their careers and this comes at a price on the market,» Luisa said. «Plus, people who come from elsewhere are paid a premium because of the risk they take by changing companies, just like you are now. But as I said before, at Microsoft you are appreciated and I think that maybe you haven't read your boss correctly. Manuel is a good boss, but you've been mistaken in thinking that he is able to know what each of you is thinking, since he has 14 people under his direct supervision,» she continued. «Did you tell anyone what you were thinking? Did you speak with Manuel or with the person on my HR team who works with you?» she asked.

«No, I don't want to be a troublemaker,» Rocío responded.

«I get it. In any case, you have to understand that I have 750 people in the company and it's impossible for me to know what all of you are thinking. If you have a concern, help me do my job. Ask me for a one-on-one and we'll have coffee. It's a shame, because I think you reached mistaken conclusions on your own,» Luisa said. «The fact that a Human Resources Director at a company like this one wants to sit down with you and ask you what you want in order to stay is something that is probably never going to

7. Similar to the Management Committee.

happen to you again. Is it a matter of your team? Does it have to do with Manuel?» Luisa continued.

«No, not at all. I get along great with Manuel and the entire team. I like all of them but I've already made my decision,» Rocío said.

She left Luisa's office. The decision seemed like a done deal, and although Luisa didn't understand it, she couldn't do anything else about it. Right then, her office phone rang.

«Hi, Luisa, it's Manuel. I was calling to see if you've talked to Rocío and if you've been able to keep her,» Manuel said.

«Manuel, Rocío has shown a level of immaturity that we haven't managed properly. The trust has been broken, and this time there's no going back, but we can't let it happen again. Since the younger generations have fewer constraints, it's easier for them to switch jobs than it was for us. In the future, you have to be more attentive and manage their time better,» Luisa told him.

Did Rocío leave primarily because of Manuel's management? What measures should be taken to avoid undesired resignations? Likewise, would the managers from older generations be willing to pay more attention to the younger generations? How would the millennials that are beginning to be promoted to managerial positions do it?

Luisa was keenly aware that she was just seeing the tip of the iceberg. She wasn't sure whether it was better to let things flow the way they had been so far or assume the risks involved in adapting to the new needs. She couldn't stop thinking about the words of Vicente Del Bosque[8] that she had recently heard at a breakfast colloquium: «The biggest challenge of a trainer in the changing room is that only 11 players can go onto the pitch.»

---

8. A football coach who has won the most important trophies.

EXHIBIT

Exhibit 1
Financial Information on Microsoft

Financial Highlights (in millions, except per-share data)

Year Ended June 30,	2016	2015	2014[a]	2013	2012
Revenue	**$85,320** [a]	$93,580	$86,833	$77,849	$73,723
Gross margin	**$52,540** [a]	$60,542	$59,755	$57,464	$56,193
Operating income	**$20,182** [a][b]	$18,161 [c]	$27,759	$26,764 [e]	$21,763 [f]
Net income	**$16,798** [a][b]	$12,193 [c]	$22,074	$21,863 [e]	$16,978 [f]
Diluted earnings per share	**$2.10** [a][b]	$1.48 [c]	$2.63	$2.58 [e]	$2.00 [f]
Cash dividends declared per share	**$1.44**	$1.24	$1.12	$0.92	$0.80
Cash, cash equivalents, and short-term investments	**$113,240**	$96,526	$85,709	$77,022	$63,040
Total assets	**$193,694**	$174,472 [g]	$170,675 [g]	$140,962 [g]	$119,388 [g]
Long-term obligations	**$62,340**	$44,742 [g]	$35,391 [g]	$24,601 [g]	$20,337 [g]
Stockholders' equity	**$71,977**	$80,083	$89,784	$78,944	$66,363

Microsoft Income Statements (in millions, except per-share amounts)

Year Ended June 30	2016	2015	2014
Revenue:			
Product	$61,502	$75,956	$72,948
Service and other	$23,818	$17,624	$13,885
Total revenue	$85,320	$93,580	$86,833
Cost of revenue			
Product	$17,880	$21,410	$16,681
Service and other	$14,900	$11,628	$10,397
Total cost of revenue	$32,780	$33,038	$27,078
Gross margin	$52,540	$60,542	$59,755
Research and development	$11,988	$12,046	$11,381
Sales and marketing	$14,697	$15,713	$15,811
General and administrative	$4,563	$4,611	$4,677
Impairment, integration, and restructuring	$1,110	$10,011	$127
Operating income	$20,182	$18,161	$27,759
Other income (expense), net	−$431	$346	$61
Income before income taxes	$19,751	$18,507	$27,820
Provision for income taxes	$2,953	$6,314	$5,746
Net income	$16,798	$12,193	$22,074
Earnings per share:			
Basic	$2.12	$1.49	$2.66
Diluted	$2.10	$1.48	$2.63
Weighted average shares outstanding:			
Basic	7,925	8,177	8,299
Diluted	8,013	8,254	8,399
Cash dividends declared per common share	$1.44	$1.24	$1.12

Source: https://www.microsoft.com/investor/reports/ar16/index.html, last accessed July 2017.

EXHIBIT 2
Microsoft's Competition

Market Consolidation (in millions of dollars)

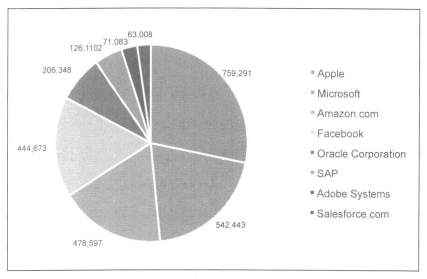

Source: Prepared by authors based on information from Thomson ONE.

Exhibit 3

Financial Information on Microsoft Ibérica (in thousands of euros)

Profit and Loss Statement	2016	2015	2014	2013	2012	2011	2010
Net turnover	180,640	166,691	167,835	170,014	159,852	157,625	155,533
Operating profit	19,492	16,535	13,919	13,375	14,916	14,481	17,416
Financial income	51	326	133	126	711	577	433
Financial expenses	80	118	29	11	14	0.19	95
Financial performance	–29	207	103	115	697	577	337
Ordinary pre-tax profits	19,463	16,743	14,023	13,490	15,614	15,058	17,753
Corporate tax	7,452	6,722	5,644	5,425	6,117	6,136	6,666
Income from ordinary activities	12,010	10,021	8,378	8,065	9,497	8,922	11,087
Annual balance	12,010	10,021	8,378	8,065	9,497	8,922	11,087
Personnel costs	95,118	89,656	82,908	84,236	79,846	77,965	79,029
Provision for depreciation of assets	1,855	1,193	505	1,632	1,038	967	883
Financial and similar expenses	54	118	10	11	0.70	0.19	69
Cash flow	13,866	11,214	8,883	9,697	10,535	9,890	11,971
Added value	116,492	107,712	97,447	99,370	96,500	93,992	97,736
EBIT	19,492,405	16,535,887	13,919,705	13,375,479	14,916,989	14,481,842	17,416,120
EBITDA	21,348,386	17,729,298	14,425,081	15,007,645	15,955,001	15,449,340	18,299,728

Source: Prepared by the authors based on data from SABI.

EXHIBIT 4

Employees of Microsoft Ibérica

	2016	2015	2014	2013	2012	2011	2010	2009
Males	445	431	435	449	474	468	464	490
Females	264	225	190	186	183	179	178	187
Total	709	656	625	635	657	647	642	677
% women	37.24%	34.30%	30.40%	29.29%	27.85%	27.67%	27.73%	27.62%

Source: Prepared by the authors based on data provided by the company.

EXHIBIT 5

Management Committee of Microsoft Ibérica

Pilar López Álvarez
President of Microsoft España

Saoirse Fahey
Marketing and Operations Director

Ana Alonso Muñumer
Director of Large Businesses and
Partnerships

Gonzalo Díe
Public Sector Director

Rafael Sanz
Director of the Division of Businesses
and Partnerships of Microsoft Ibérica

Carolina Castillo
Consumer Division Director

Tiago Monteiro
Director of the Services Division
of Microsoft Ibérica

Ángel Sáenz de Cenzano
Director of the Platform,
Development and Innovation
Division of Microsoft Ibérica

Ignacio Panizo
Financial Director

Luisa Izquierdo
Director of Human Resources of
Microsoft Ibérica

Carlos de la Iglesia
Director of Communication of
Microsoft Ibérica

Source: https://www.microsoft.com/investor/reports/ar16/index.html, last accessed July 2017.

EXHIBIT 6

MACH Participants' Areas of Expertise

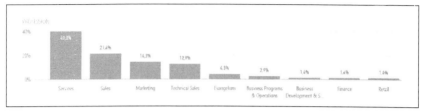

Source: Information provided by the company.

EXHIBIT 7

The MACH Experience

Source: Information provided by the company.

Chapter 8

Clara at Salesforce Europe: Adapting to a New Culture

Friday

It was 4pm. After a tough work week, Sandra[1] was dying to go home and rest, but she still had to wrap up a few things. Meanwhile, she was thinking about what he had witnessed that morning. Suddenly, after a year and a half of working beautifully together, Clara and Juan, two of the most promising young employees to join their team of late, no longer wanted to work together. They informed her after a heated argument, in which the two shouted insults at one another.

Since she arrived in Dublin as manager of the Pre-sales team, Sandra, faithful to the company's corporate culture, had to deal with the personal problems of her employees, while orienting and redirecting their career. Despite having someone with whom she could share her own problems, she did not do so as regularly as the members of the new generation had grown accustomed to doing with her. Would this trend continue to increase? If so, it would have to be effectively worked into the management of her time in order to maintain the upward curve in achieving the business results expected of her and her team.

---

1. Names have been changed to maintain confidentiality.

Salesforce

Salesforce was founded in 1999 by a group of former Oracle executives led by Marc Benioff. Their mission was to reinvent customer relationship management (CRM). At present, Salesforce has over 25,000 employees and nearly $10 billion in revenue. It offers a global and integrated solution to manage.all interactions with customers, which is designed to help organizations grow successfully. Its products are fully cloud integrated, which cuts nearly all setup and maintenance costs and allows users to manage their customer relationships from anywhere they have access to the Internet. When Salesforce started up, the industry was said to be in a golden period, as Marc Benioff had experienced in the 1990s. CRM is an essential part of a strategy to manage all the relationships and interactions between companies and their current and potential customers, and ultimately raise their profitability. In addition to increasing marketing quality, boosting sales and improving customer service, it also facilitates supply chain management.

The initial products offered by Salesforce to help organizations achieve greater growth and success were: Sales Cloud, designed to increase sales and revenue; Service Cloud, which assists customers through any channel from anywhere with a platform that allows them to maintain communication with companies; Marketing Cloud, which lets companies create personalized marketing campaigns via email, mobile, social media, websites, etc.; Analytics Cloud, which enables users to explore their data, quickly find answers and immediately take action; Community Cloud, an online self-service community that helps customers, partners and employees find the information they need; Salesforce Platform, created to help organizations maximize the power of CRM; and Salesforce IoT[2], which gives users a more comprehensive view of the their customers' behavior by connecting any device, sensor, website or interaction with Salesforce applications.

The company established its headquarters in Ireland. Due to the tax benefits offered by that country, it is not the only tech company going that route: Oracle, Microsoft and SAP also located their European headquarters near Dublin. Despite belonging to the European Union, some aspects of day-to-day life and the climate diminish the attractiveness for professionals to relocate to the island. However, many young people, especially Europeans, use it as a place where they can study and improve

---

2. Internet of Things (IoT): term describing the interconnection of everyday objects with the Internet.

their level of English. Although this flow happens, particularly in holiday periods, many Europeans spend a semester in Ireland or start their careers there, looking to increase their chances of finding work when they return to their countries of origin.

Corporate culture and employee management

At the time Salesforce was formed, the market situation (see Exhibit 1) was such that companies were competing not only in price and quality, but also in recruiting and retaining talent. Life inside the company is governed by the values known as ohana, which means «family» in Hawaiian. The values of trust, growth, innovation, equality, customer success, transparency, well-being and happiness make Salesforce a special company for its employees. «Many companies tout their 'work hard, play hard' culture, but at Salesforce, there's not actually a division between when I'm working hard and when I'm having fun,» says the head of the Employee Success Department. From the first moment of the selection process (evaluated positively by 77% of the candidates—see Exhibit 2), it seeks to make the applicant feel special.

«At my previous company, they acted like piranhas; here, at Salesforce, we're all about building stable and lasting relationships with clients. If you see that something is not going to be useful for them, your bosses tell you not to sell it,» a veteran manager had told Clara when she joined.

The fixed salaries at each level are slightly higher than those of the market. Likewise, workers can earn a very substantial percentage bonus by obtaining results and achieving team goals (however, as a former employee posted online, «It was hard, sometimes impossible, to hit the quotas»). They have other perks as well, like pension plans, social benefits, courses, paid time off for volunteering, a gym with massages included, and assistance to quit smoking or engage in hobbies. Salesforce expects employees to manage their own schedules and calendars, and organizes attractive trips for those who excel in sales. Salesforce executives take pride in belonging to one of the most highly valued companies in the market (see Exhibit 3), which often appears on the lists of best places to work. The challenge is to maintain the commitment of all employees, especially new hires, who have extremely high expectations.

«I left my previous company because money was the only thing that mattered. When I turned in my letter of resignation, they asked me why I was leaving, and how much I wanted to be paid. They couldn't understand that the problem wasn't money—it was the whole corporate culture and its values,» said Ana, head of Business Development Representation (BDR).

According to the opinion repeatedly expressed in town halls and corporate meetings, succeeding Salesforce requires an ambitious, proactive, tenacious person with a very positive attitude. The idea of opening a market by understanding the needs of companies and proposing the necessary solution to achieve better customer management is a shared motivation among managers who have been with the company for some years.

All employees are treated equally: they all have the same computer and cellphone, and nobody has a company car or office. «If I start to lose motivation or receive offers from other organizations, I can ask to change positions or projects, but not a salary increase,» Clara told her former colleagues and friends. In the Employee Success Department, they have weekly recruitment meetings, where managers discuss problems affecting their teams and inform the group if anyone wants to leave the company, in order to make decisions and carry them out.

Clara on Sandra's Pre-sales team

In the Irish capital, Sandra headed up the Pre-sales team, which Clara and Juan had joined just six months prior. In addition to this core team, Salesforce had regional offices in many European countries. The company was in a period of expansion and growth. Although most employees resided in Dublin, in recent years the number of workers in Spain had gone from 5 to 130, and the trend continued.

The Pre-sales team was built on three core values: commitment to the customer, tangible results and the development of future account executives. «If they work in Pre-sales, it is clear that they will be good professionals and get promoted; but if they are not good in that initial stage, they will most likely be asked to leave,» said Sandra.

Now, a brief description of the protagonists of this case:

Sandra

Sandra Zafra, 38 years old, was an enterprising woman, full of hope and vitality that was contagious among her teams. In 1998, she started her undergraduate studies in English Language and Literature at the University of Sevilla, graduating in 2004. Subsequently, she traveled to the United States to earn the Certificate of Online Learning and Foreign Language Acquisition at the University of North Carolina, where she began to develop her affinity for technology and its applications. Before landing at Salesforce, where she served as manager for the Iberian and Italian markets, she completed three master's degrees at universities in the United States, Europe and Asia, and gained considerable experience. From 2002 to 2016, she had worked for a total of 13 companies, one of which she founded herself. Sandra felt her extensive experience helped her understand customers' needs and adapt to them. After several years in Dublin, she was ready to move to Madrid.

Ana

At 36, Ana Recio was highly motivated to achieve the business objectives that she had set out. According to her boss, «she had tremendous energy, which she combined with her team spirit and strong ability to manage teams.» From 2000 to 2005, she studied Business Administration and Management while working in the Sales Department of a multinational consumer goods company. After finishing her studies, she started working for a multinational competitor of Salesforce, a company that she left after more than eight years in various positions in the Sales Department. At Salesforce, she had just taken on new responsibilities as BDR manager and was looking to continue advancing her professional career, but she felt achieving her objectives meant focusing on recruiting, developing and leading talent: if her teammates were successful, that meant she would be also.

Clara

Clara Barrios was 28 years old and, although she had arrived in Ireland a year and a half ago, she was still getting used to the cold, disagreeable weather, which was a little easier thanks to her Galician origin. Her previous experience in Microsoft's Human Resources Department had helped her understand the needs of organizations in the industry. She felt comfortable in dealing with customers and appreciated the possibilities that Salesforce offered its employees, especially regarding flexibility and travel. Her university colleagues highlighted her «responsibility, proactivity and enthusiastic contribution to the team,» as well as «her curiosity to always learn more than what was in the books and how highly demanding she was on herself.»

Juan

Juan Ortiz, a 28-year-old computer scientist, had arrived in Ireland shortly before Clara and, given his Andalusian blood, it was even harder for him to get used to the cloudy, rainy weather. After finishing his degree in Business Administration and Management and doing internships in the Sales Department of an agricultural company, he decided to travel to Ireland to improve his English. He had started working at Salesforce 15 months prior.

Beginnings at PSA-Citroën

The good grades Clara earned doing her Economics and Business Administration degree set her up for a position in the Human Resources department of the PSA Group factory in Vigo (Pontevedra), one of the most efficient in the world. There she learned everything from managing salaries to union relationships, and how to handle high levels of labor unrest—one of the most prominent issues within the company. Two years later, after the company was forced to close factories around the world, it began to relocate workers and facilitate employee departures. Clara took advantage of the opportunity to fulfill a long-cherished desire: to earn an MBA. During her studies, Clara improved her already solid level of English and built her network in forums for human resources professionals in Madrid. In the process, she met the heads of the department at Microsoft, with whom she established an excellent relationship. Her proactivity and initiative surprised the company's directors, so they offered her a job when she graduated.

Microsoft

At Microsoft, Clara enjoyed the dynamic nature of the industry and its desire to promote cultural change and excellence in the management and training of employees. Progressively, although indirectly, she started gaining experience with clients, and realized that she loved the intensity of that close-up, daily interaction. Given her personal commitment, she soon set her sights on a loftier role, one that would give her a chance to have an international experience and engage in sales activities. As Clara explains:

«I had been at the company for seven or eight months when I started thinking about leaving. I had expectations that were not being met, and Human Resources was telling me that, in the medium term, I should stay in my role. In my department, I was stuck and had no shot at promotion. Nor could I get into other departments that would fulfill my interests, such as Sales.»

Microsoft sent Clara to an event to attract professionals in Barcelona. At that time, Salesforce was already a company known for having very good workers and giving them quality training. Out of curiosity, Clara took the opportunity to approach the Salesforce position by posing as a university senior. «I went into stealth mode. I covered all the Microsoft stuff I was carrying and went over to the Salesforce booth out of curiosity, to see what they were offering both at personal level and the differences compared to my company, one of their competitors,» said Clara. They explained to her in an attractive way what Salesforce was and, after acknowledging her lack of sales experience, they let her know that it was not essential, as long as she showed she had the necessary skills. The open-mindedness of the Salesforce staff inspired Clara to try to make a place for herself.

«I ended up coming clean and telling them that I was coming from Microsoft, but I told them that what they offered really interested me. I think what they liked about me was my ability to approach someone who, in theory, didn't need me and wasn't looking for me, in order to sell myself.»

After a few days, they contacted her through LinkedIn to start a selection process. As Clara describes it:

«I decided to participate out of curiosity to know what a company with such a good reputation was offering and see what its policies of attracting and retaining talent were, since I was the one being attracted. When I did interviews with Salesforce executives and managers, I was fascinated.»

Selection process and beginning at Salesforce

«They offered me everything that I could think of, especially international experience and a structured and fast-moving career path,» Clara said in explaining her decision to leave Microsoft. «I also liked the kind of interviews they did: they were more strategic than I was used to. Sandra not only offered me a job, but it was also evident that she was going to help me improve my social skills, which I knew were poor.»

Salesforce began meeting Clara's expectations:

«From the first moment, you set goals and deadlines to achieve them. I have accomplished them all, and when I have done so earlier than planned, I have been rewarded, both financially and with wonderful travel experiences and promotions; the way they take care of me is one of the aspects that motivates me the most.»

Regarding the need to move to Ireland, Clara explained: «To this day, I keep in touch with former colleagues, and many ask me about working at Salesforce and the conditions. In the end, something that turns many of them off is having to go to Ireland.» She admitted that arriving in the country was hard, since culturally it is very different from Spain. But the activities Salesforce organized to integrate their employees helped to get past that initial barrier:

> «We end up becoming workaholics, since we are very young people living away from our family and spending a lot of time with colleagues outside work because there are lots of activities, from charity events to dinners organized by the company and sporting events.»

These activities, along with the fast career path and the possibility of returning to Spain in good standing with the same company, compensated for the initial difficulty in adapting to the country.

One of the hallmarks of Salesforce is that closeness among employees is encouraged in every country where it has offices, although Clara witnessed its less positive consequences: «It is true that closeness means that work conversation does not end when we leave the office... it continues when we're having a beer.»

Career plans in Pre-sales

The members of the Pre-sales team had career plans that helped them climb the ladder within the company as they achieved the objectives established at each step. Meritocracy allowed good employees to move up the organization faster, at their own individual pace. They started as interns or business development associates (BDA); from there, they became sales development representatives (SDR) and then business development representatives (BDR), before ending up as account executives, a position where they became specialized according to the type of business they wanted to focus on or, on the contrary, they could move toward manager positions (see Exhibit 4).

Both SDRs and BDRs spent most of their working hours on the phone. SDRs were in charge of managing incoming calls. The four pillars of the professionals in the Sales Development Team were: alignment with the Marketing team, daily rigor, rapid response and persistence, and alignment with sales. «Six is the magic number of calls before giving up with a client,» they repeated in the courses. «However, very few representatives try to contact more than twice,» acknowledged the company's training managers. Their performance was measured according to their daily, weekly and monthly key performance indicators (KPI), which included making 60 calls a day.

> «The phone part is really hard,» Sandra acknowledged. «That's why at Salesforce we offer a lot of coaching and a lot of training.» This training included Bootcamp, where the company's new professionals spent a full week. «When working over the phone, it is very important to know how to communicate and have a clear methodology. Because of this, generalist profiles with thorough training in the sales methodology usually work very well.»

Meanwhile, BDRs were in charge of generating new opportunities and had to be aligned with the regional vice presidents. The account executives coordinated a group of specialists from the Sales team. Although they needed to have extensive knowledge about the product, the teams had specialized techies in the field. As Sandra emphasized: «This is about people rather than technology.»

When asked about integrating new generations in the company's sales processes, Sandra explained:

> «We can't put millennials on the phone to try to sell products and services to the customer while behaving naturally, because they would be too informal: they don't know the hierarchy to speak properly with a manager or CEO.»

To achieve this adaptation, Salesforce professionals carried out training based on the Sandler methodology (see Exhibit 5). This methodology was structured to guide the sales process, and covered everything from how to begin when the salesperson picks up the phone to how to talk with a secretary, pick and use the first 20 words, and organize the questions in a conversation. By doing this, improvisation was avoided when generating sales.

The training and the use of this methodology allowed them to gain the maximum amount of information in a conversation with the client. The questions were intended to detect if there was a sales opportunity using three levels: technical, business and personal. According to Sandra:

> «Millennials are very good at asking questions at the technical level, about technology and the tools that customers use. The business ones they

do relatively well with, though they may occasionally forget some of them. But the questions they really struggle with are the personal ones.»

As she told her sales teams: «If you don't know why the project is important for the customer, you don't know what their degree of engagement will be.»

To give feedback to salespeople and improve their conversations with customers, the company had established express coaching, which consisted of meetings between managers and employees that did not last more than five minutes. Beforehand, the manager listened to some of the conversations held by members of the Sales team and then cited them in a meeting room to ask what could have been done better.

The manager-coach role

Coaching was one of the main obligations of managers, who after being appointed started a learning program with multiple internal training courses. In addition, they had €5,000 a year available for additional training, which Sandra had taken advantage of to do an online professional coaching program. One of the central themes addressed during the training was how to find, motivate and retain talent. According to Sandra, a major challenge was the need to make younger employees understand that they must know how to wait to achieve their goals and progress in the organization. «They look directly into the future and do not realize what they have in front of their eyes. I have the feeling that they want to reach the top without climbing the mountain,» she lamented when asked about the difference between the different generations. «They think they know everything; but they often seem narcissistic and arrogant. Before reaching a lofty position, they have to develop commitment. They see positions as more short-term than previous generations.» At Salesforce, the expectations of the new generations are managed by managers through conversations, which practically turns professional relationships into personal ones.

> «Millennials tend to be smart and well prepared academically, but sometimes they are immature both in their behaviors and the approaches they propose. The young ladies are more responsible, mature and effective. The young men tend to compete; they seem to have the need to show their superiority,» Ana commented to Sandra.
> «It's true: they want to achieve everything quickly and without responsibilities. In their mind, there is nowhere to go but up. Plus, managing them requires weekly conversations for them to feel encouraged to share their problems and concerns,» Sandra replied.

To do this, Salesforce managers used to create what they called «safe environments,» where the concerns shared by employees did not leave the room. Managers took advantage of the time to talk about their job expectations and the future that the company could offer them, while trying to gain valuable insights into how to motivate and retain them. As Clara acknowledged: «Sometimes, Sandra has been more than a manager for me. We've had conversations that were really therapeutic counseling sessions.» And, as Sandra explains: «With Clara, we had talked about her future and what she would do in my department a year before she joined it.»

Managers who progressed in Salesforce had an open mind. According to a Dutch account executive, «as a member of the team, you can tell them your concerns and they get personally involved to find a solution. At Salesforce, managers listen to you and respond.» She continued: «I've seen companies where they listen to you and comfort you, but they don't react or look for a solution.» An American manager acknowledged that «not all managers were equally engaged, but those who did could get where they wanted within the company. It was something that one had to earn person to person.»

Although it was not formally written, there were also certain approaches that worked better than others; it was known that participating in certain projects and with certain departments helped a person structure and create the political image needed to move forward. «If you want to advance, being good doesn't cut it; you have to prove it. In that regard, it's the same as my previous company,» said Clara, who invested time and effort in creating and promoting her own image. Working hard, achieving the required results and showing her value was important when establishing her own personal brand. Sharing the successes and achieving them at the multifunctional level was one of the strategies used by Clara to make herself known, since she had always believed that shared success was sweeter.

To prevent people from becoming frustrated in positions where more experience was needed before moving on to the next level of responsibility, managers improved employee training. Clara said that «I had very narrow goals, and Sandra helped me expand them by taking on more projects. Instead of getting promoted in six months, I would take a year, but I knew that those projects made me more complete.» The young woman added that she trusted her boss.

However, the person in charge of Clara would become Ana, since she would go from selling to startups to doing it with large corporations. According to Clara, «this step was necessary to continue growing as a professional. Depending on the customer, everything is different: the conversations, the sales speech, how you look at the numbers, knowledge of the industry....» To learn the details about customers, sales managers relied on their most experienced teammates.

The perspective of the younger generation

> «I hate micromanagement, where bosses are all over you when you don't hit the targets and they go from being monthly to weekly or even daily, to keep closer tabs on you. It doesn't help me: it frustrates me,» said Catherine, a 25-year-old Czech worker who studied marketing and had been with the company for a year and a half.

For Martin, a 29-year-old German computer scientist, the feeling of being «stuck» in a position without the ability to change the situation on his own or with the help of his boss, who forced him to continue doing the same thing without being able to learn new things, would lead him to look for a job elsewhere. That is why he accepted the Salesforce offer almost two years ago.

Eugenie, a 23-year-old employee from Grenoble who had studied economics and had been with the company for six months, said: «The most important thing is for my manager to defend me. If I'm having a bad month, I like for my manager to help me and not pressure me; and if I want to change, my manager should help me, not hinder me.»

Clara had repeatedly heard that the company's culture was fostered and encouraged teamwork. However, after a while, it seemed to her that the compensation system focused on results, and with a large variable component it created high levels of pressure. Employees felt pressured by the expectations they had of themselves, those of their boss and (no less intense) what their colleagues might think if someone went below their targets. This policy was used throughout the industry.

She recalled that in her first month in the role of business developer for large companies, after having worked in the startups segment, they allowed her to hit just 50% of the targets; in the second month, 80%; and in the third, they already demanded 100% of the required targets from everyone in that position. Her plans included changing roles once she had been at it for 15 months.

She could not get her mind off what was happening to her coworker Alexandre, a 26-year-old Israeli man who was in a rut personally and professionally before the end of his first year. His manager in Sales Development, Paul, a demanding 37-year-old Englishman with a lengthy career in sales, began a micromanagement process and started to monitor his performance on a weekly basis. Then, seeing that the trend did not change, he started doing it daily, and asked him frequently: «Why aren't you making it?» Team members knew that if someone went into a micro-management process, it would always reveal deficiencies and things that could be done better. In the end, they took it as a disturbing audit.

In the case of Alexandre, he seemingly did not hit his targets because it took him longer than his colleagues to do the same thing, which hurt his efficiency and made it impossible to reach his variable and that of his colleagues. There was also a market factor: for political reasons, everything in the region had slowed down.

The manager's warning was immediate: «If we don't rectify the trend, we will have to work more.» Alexandre responded by saying that, as soon as he was better, everything would be fine again. But his colleagues did not quite understand why he was not hitting his targets. There were those who reproached him: «My girlfriend also left, and I don't like living in Dublin either»; others were ready to lend a hand, some because he was right next to them, and others out of team spirit, while others did so because by helping him, they helped themselves. They listened to him and encouraged him when they got together outside of work, something they did almost every day, and also during the activities organized by the company on weekends. Despite people's positive inclination, Clara noticed how the atmosphere of friendship and closeness between them was deteriorating, since some people ignored the problem. It was known that either Alexandre would change, or everyone would pay, starting with Paul.

Paul reorganized Alexandre's daily schedule, hour by hour, following the example of a top performer from another team. Whereas before he had made 30 calls, he now gave him a target of 50. And he insisted: «Decide what you are going to do in each moment to improve.» Clara sensed the tension her coworker was experiencing, that he was willing to try, although he was not comfortable and the plan did not seem right.

Paul got deeply involved, taking it as a personal challenge. Clara wondered what Paul's motives were: Did he care about Alexandre or was he just interested in finding a quick solution? That doubt had come up for her in similar situations with other managers.

She also had just seen how Pascaline, a 40-year-old French manager with a partner and no children, who was very well-known in the company, had helped her and two other colleagues in an internal competition to decide the best sales improvement project, which they had won. The impact of Pascaline was enormously relational, since she was willing to help with sympathy and efficiency for as many hours as necessary. It was said that «it was a joy to work with her,» and everyone knew that at Salesforce, which was part of her personal brand. Why had she become so involved in something that brought her no direct benefit?

Although there were differences between managers in southern Europe and those in the north (according to Clara, the former were closer and less hierarchical, while the latter were more technical and structured), they all shared common cultural tendencies, including being results-oriented and their dedication, sometimes almost paternal, to the members of their teams. Clara commented:

> «I admire my managers, but I do not know if I would be willing to pay the price it takes to reach that position. Staying in Ireland does mean having more job options (and often, more promising ones); however, I prefer to occupy a lesser role or a slower career path if I can go back to my country. I come from a region where I have been taught that family, rest and food are almost a religion. At this time in my life, I have decided to keep up the fast pace and dive into my work with the goal of climbing fast professionally. However, in the future, when I have a family, I don't know if I will be able to go on like this. Of course, I have colleagues who are perfectly capable of combining everything, and I will try to find out how to do it and I will be tenacious. But I'm not willing to sacrifice having a family that I can devote myself to—more than to work—or being able to enjoy my life in general (leisure, travel... whatever you spend your money on), just to get a better position.»

The months spent at Salesforce had been very intense; Clara barely had a moment to stop and think. However, she was now aware that she and her colleagues were not very clear about what they wanted: «We're ambitious, but no one has long-term goals. We lack strategy and perseverance.» She knew she liked Sandra as a manager.

Generational differences

At Salesforce, finding the right talent was the first goal. As Sandra and Ana confessed, «getting young professionals, with the characteristics and ambition desired by the company and willing to work in Ireland, was a headache for management. Therefore, if someone of a certain level leaves, it is very difficult to fill their position.»

The growth that the organization was experiencing in recent years had created opportunities for internal growth for many employees, but it had also led to a mass hiring of foreign talent. Managing and coordinating them was a key job for managers. The Human Resources department stated:

«There are often situations in which employees 25 years of age must teach the company culture to people over 30, while the latter teach them about the experience of having worked with customers for years. Getting this kind of collaboration is not always easy, because frictions and misunderstandings constantly arise.»

Juan explained:

«I would only leave Salesforce if something negative happened internally, such as if expectations started to go unmet, or an outside project came up that attracted me more. It is a great company where you learn a lot, but there are very interesting projects at startups where the impact of your work is greater despite receiving lower compensation. It would frustrate me to stop learning.»

For many Salesforce employees, being participants in an interesting project where they could make the biggest contributions was so important that it led them to accept positions with startups. Although salaries at those companies tended to be lower, this was compensated for by the job title and the importance of their role within the team.

«When I've worked with people of our generation, it's been easier. I think we're more like the generations that precede us than the millennials. We were told something and we did it, we had patience to achieve long-term goals and we persevered until we achieved them,» Sandra told the manager of her department, a 42-year-old Irish woman.

«Yes, I also believe that the new generation switches jobs without qualms; young people are not retained out of loyalty. They move fast, work their tails off, but they abandon it midway with the same enthusiasm and start off on another project. It's as if they started so hard that their own momentum made them fall,» responded the manager.

«Besides, we had a more defined concept of «friendship» and «coworker»; they constantly mix the two, and that makes it hard to manage the team,» added Sandra.

Managers with more experience often commented that the most complicated task in the company was to separate their work from the rest of their lives; in other words, finding a balance between personal and professional life did not seem to be a real priority for many of them. «It's easy to focus on work and accounts, and that affects your personal life after working hours and consumes time on weekends,» a former employee posted online.

A personal or business conflict

Clara received a call from her mother to see how she was doing after returning from a week of working in Galicia: «How is your week going in Ireland?»

«Everything's fine. You know, there's always a lot of work, but the atmosphere in the office is very good. Yesterday, when we left, we went out for drinks, and we're thinking of visiting the Ring of Kerry some weekend. Also, if we manage to coordinate our vacations, we are also planning to show the rest of the team around Spain.»

After hanging up the phone, Clara reflected. During her time in Ireland, she had met many people and had developed good friendships with many of them. However, she spent most of her time with colleagues on the Salesforce team. They were the ones she made plans with and called when she needed moral support or someone to let her vent. Her attitude was not an isolated practice. The cultural values that aimed to turn Salesforce into a family, the long workdays and the employees' involvement with personal and team success did the rest. It was also not uncommon to see two coworkers at the company start dating.

«Once again, you are behind on your targets. So, there is no way we can reach the team quota this month,» Clara blurted out to Juan. «You only care about the quota and going on trips,» her colleague retorted.

Sandra attentively watched this argument, which became increasingly heated, until spiraling into reproaches of each other's character and attacking one another with information that could only come from a relationship that extended beyond the office. Nevertheless, she preferred not to intervene, since she realized that the pressure among team members to reach the team quota was normal and should not escalate any further, nor did it appear that would happen. However, the week went by, and what had started as a professional argument was becoming a serious situation. That Friday, they both came to her office. The rush to close the month on a good note was evident.

Clara, with a certain tone of desperation in her words, explained: «Sandra, I can't work with Juan anymore; with colleagues who do so little for the common goal, you can't get anywhere. He lacks the desire.»

For his part, Juan told her, resentfully: «It's impossible to work with Clara. She only cares about herself and nothing else matters. She only thinks about getting promoted.»

Sandra decided to wait.

Friday

Before shutting down her computer and going home, Sandra began to ponder how she could keep progressing with her professional career when so many issues required her energy and attention. Being aware of the problems, anticipating some of the conflicts and coming up with attractive projects for each of her colleagues was a daily struggle. There began to be increasingly more cases of employees who found more appealing opportunities at startups. Until now, she had unhesitatingly acted as a safety net for those above and below her, to protect the team while trying to prevent internal problems from arising. Although the company's culture formally validated her approach, she began to see more and more managers whose main performance criteria ignored anything other than results.

Her boyfriend had left Ireland months ago for work reasons; she wanted to return to Spain with a good position. The next day she would go to the Cliffs of Moher.

EXHIBIT

EXHIBIT 1
Market Capitalization

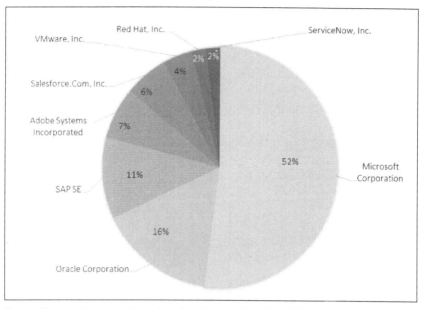

Source: Prepared by the authors, based on data obtained from Thomson One.

EXHIBIT 2
Selection Process

Source: Glassdoor, Inc. 2008-2018. Glassdoor website. [Online]. [Last accessed November 15, 2017]. Available at: https://www.glassdoor.com/Reviews/Salesforce-Reviews-E11159.htm.

Exhibit 3
Statistics and Ratings on Salesforce

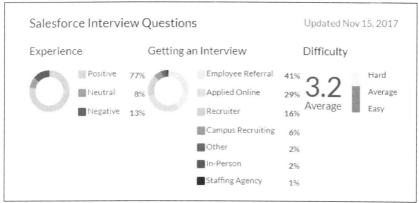

Source: Glassdoor, Inc. 2008-2018. Glassdoor website. [Online]. [Last accessed November 15, 2017]. Available at: https://www.glassdoor.com/Reviews/Salesforce-Reviews-E11159.htm

Exhibit 4
Career Path

Position	Time	Salary*
Business development associate (BDA)	0-6 months	16-28,000
Sales development representative (SDR)	10-12 months	48,000
Business development representative (BDR)	12-18 months	58,000
Account executive	Around 2 years	50-90,000
Manager		87-94,000

(*) Estimated salaries in euros according to industry executives consulted by the authors.
Source: Prepared by the authors

Exhibit 5
The Sandler methodology[3]

There are three basic principles of the Sandler methodology: translate, transform and train. The attitudes and abilities of the sellers have to be translated into defined and measurable actions. Attitudes are transformed to achieve personal, departmental and corporate goals. Finally, training in this methodology allows sellers to develop competently, efficiently and effectively.

The objectives of Sandler training are to restructure the business development efforts and establish relevant and quantifiable objectives, implement a framework of activities to quickly detect quality opportunities and decide where and with whom to invest time.

Meanwhile, the sales process is divided into three phases: The first is to create and maintain a comfortable atmosphere for doing business. Among other things, it is about connecting, communicating and controlling; in the second phase, the goal is to qualify everything from the degree of affinity between the problem and the solution being offered, to the budget; the last step is the closing of the sale or «no sale.» It is about hitting the targets and carrying out after-sales follow-up.

3. Information obtained from the Sandler website: http://www.costarica.sandler.com

Chapter 9

American Valley

For Louis Stevenson, a promising employee of American Valley's technology division, it was not going to be an easy interview[1]. Louis worked as a senior analyst on sales platform projects, reporting to a project manager. His main tasks included process and application certification, test case design, test cycle planning, and monitoring report generation, all this as the head of a small team of four junior analysts. In his four years with the company he had made solid progress. In the first two years he had earned his stripes as a junior analyst, had completed a master's degree in finance, banking and insurance, and was now starting to informally take on certain general management functions, which usually was seen as a positive sign with respect to future promotion.

That morning, however, Louis was going to be seeing Sandra Paulson, the human resources business partner for his area, to whom he had already announced over the phone his intention to leave the firm. The offer he had accepted from another company was very attractive, but American Valley was not the kind of company that people left of their own choice. More worryingly, Louis did not see how he could avoid having to talk about difficulties he had been having with his boss, and that made him uncomfortable, as he did not like to speak badly of anyone. On

---

1. The names have been changed to preserve confidentiality.

entering the meeting room he found, to his surprise, that Sandra was not alone. With her was Martha Weird, human resources director of the technology division, with whom Louis had established a relationship of some trust during his four years with the company.

Martha: Please come in, Louis. How are you?

Louis: Ready for a change, as I already indicated to Sandra. This is a surprise, seeing you here!

Martha: When Sandra told me about your concerns, I asked her if I could sit in on this meeting today. People like you are the ones who add value to this company—and it's my job to make sure everyone gets the best out of themselves. So what's this about?

Louis: Well, I imagine Sandra will have given you some idea already. Quite simply, I've had a very good offer from another company, and I feel that my time here is up. I'm very grateful for the experience I've gained over these last four years, but I think I'll develop better with the other firm. I've been asked not to disclose the name of the company I'm going to—on account of some internal issue with the person I'll be replacing—but I can assure you it's not a direct competitor. We can still be friends!

Martha: Hold on, Louis, don't be in such a hurry. We don't want this to be an exit interview. Let's make it an opportunity to share some thoughts. You never know, we may be able to come to an arrangement where you get what you're looking for here, without having to leave. I don't think your time here is up. On the contrary, there are still plenty of things for you to do. We have loads of opportunities for you, and more to come! I can't believe you'll find better conditions anywhere else. I bet we can at least match them, if not beat them.

Louis: It's not about money, Martha. I know my area inside out, whereas where I'm going they'll be giving me new things to do all the time. It will be better for me in the long run.

Martha: I wasn't talking just about pay and benefits, Louis, although we can talk about that, too, of course. What I meant was, I don't think you'll find better career development opportunities anywhere else. There's a consensus here that the technology division has an important role to play—big things are going to happen. And the group itself is huge.

	So if you're interested in other areas, just let us know and we'll give it our consideration.
Louis:	Please, Martha, not now! I've waited long enough, but none of the things I was hoping for have come my way, as Sandra knows.
Martha:	Things are changing, Louis. Let me let you in on a secret. Do you remember the high-potential «Talent Inside» project? Well, we're about to announce the assessment results, and you'll find you're in a very good position. You're one of the people chosen for the fast track. It'll be two years of very hard work, but extremely enriching. You'll rotate through three positions, do various custom training programs, and have the opportunity to join cross-organizational projects that will give you a better understanding of the company as a whole, and more visibility. And there'll be a lot of travel, too. Believe me, you won't get bored! If it's development you're looking for, I don't believe you'll find anything better.
Louis:	All this is very flattering, but I've already given them my word. And I'm not the sort of person to back out at this stage and let them down.
Martha:	We understand that perfectly well, Louis. But you don't want to spoil your chances by being too gentlemanly—there's too much at stake. It won't be the end of the world! Tell them it's my fault, tell them about the «Talent Inside» project. A couple of weeks from now I bet they'll have forgotten all about it. Of course, we can also talk about pay and benefits. I know it's not your main motive—and you'd do well to make sure they understand that—but there's no need for you to lose out financially either.
Louis:	I can't do it, Martha. Honestly, they've treated me very well, which I can't say has always been the case here. I can't do that to them, they don't deserve it. Also, the development plans they've told me about may not be so dramatic, but they start on day one. You are being completely straight with me, aren't you?
Martha:	Of course I am!
Louis:	Well I'll be straight with you, then. You see, I guessed I'd do well in the talent analysis. At times I've felt I was being wasted here. But we've had to have a special project and an outside consultant called in to do an assessment before

anything started to be done about it. And that's not the only thing. You know I find my boss very difficult and am thoroughly fed up with him. But it's not just me—it's the whole floor. You have no idea how pleased I'll be not to have anything more to do with him! I think a good project manager carries ultimate responsibility for the planning and execution of a project, so he needs to have all the risks under control and reduce uncertainty to a minimum. What I mean is that open communication should be an absolute priority. But with him it's the opposite. I'm sorry to have to say this, but with people like him in senior positions you can invest as much as you like in projects such as «Talent Inside», but it won't do much good.

Martha: Let's keep to the subject, Louis. We're not here to judge Sam Walcott. You know he's in a difficult position here. He gets a lot of pressure from higher up, and he always has his back against the wall.

Louis: That's exactly the problem, Martha. It's not just Sam. He's a particularly flagrant example, but I've come to the conclusion that if you want to get anywhere in this company, you have to follow his example: to get to the top you have to grind people down. But I'm not prepared to do that. You said earlier on that you didn't want this to be an exit interview, but let me tell you, this is a feedback opportunity that you really shouldn't miss. Just as an experiment, google the name of our company and «Sam Walcott» and see what you get. I did it last week and I could hardly believe it, even though I knew what to expect from my own experience. When I accepted the preliminary offer from the other firm, I felt relieved to be getting away from all that. There's no question about it, my time here is up.

The AVI Group

Headquartered in California, the AVI group is one of the world's largest insurance companies, with a particularly strong presence in the U.S. and Canada, Latin America, the United Kingdom, the Scandinavian countries, and the Iberian Peninsula. The company employs more than 42,000 people, roughly half of whom work in the U.S. and Canada, and the rest in the other countries, in which the group embarked on a rapid expansion fifteen years ago (see **Exhibit 1**).

The product portfolio covers practically every area of insurance, as well as the management of mutual funds and pension funds and plans in various countries. In 2010 the group posted gross revenue of more than 1.7 billion dollars and had total assets of 56 billion (see **Exhibit 2**).

Strategic priorities for the AVI group are to expand internationally and improve operational efficiency by creating synergies. As a step toward improving operational efficiency, a few years ago the group created the technology companies division, whose main responsibilities are integrated systems and shared services.

AVI has a view of systems that goes beyond technology to include all the software applications, operating models and organized processes that serve all the group's business areas. The underlying conviction is that technology allows AVI to deliver high quality service to its customers and create value sustainably.

The technology division carries out mainly three types of activities in three specialized companies:

- Software development and common systems integration services.
- Communications infrastructure and data processing center management for the group.
- Operations and back office services management.

The division employs around 8,000 people, with an average age of 32, mostly engineering graduates.

The Situation in the Fall of 2010: A Workforce Problem?

The AVI group has well established HR management policies that have consistently earned it top places in the best employers lists over the last five years.

Its selection policies include a wide range of recruitment sources, with significant investments in visibility in universities and postgraduate schools, backed up by rigorous competency-based selection processes. Although the general policy is to recruit young graduates who will build a career in the company, the company's growth has also created opportunities to hire in established professionals from other companies, generally using top headhunters.

Pay and benefits policies are implemented through systems that combine market-level fixed salaries with levels of variable pay that are around 20% above the market average. Variable pay is calculated based on both individual performance and company and group performance.

The group also invests heavily in training and development. Its training center in Santa Barbara sets the standard in the industry. Talent identification and development involve sophisticated 360° feedback programs, advanced job rotation and internal succession policies, and two annual projects to identify high-potential employees. The final phases of these two projects involve around 240 professionals each year, of whom around 80 are chosen to join the «high-flyer» group, who receive preferential treatment and special benefits to encourage loyalty.

Against this background, at the end of 2010 the group's HR management launched an initiative specifically to identify young talent in the technology division. Since it was first set up, practically nobody from the technology division had been selected to join AVI's high-flyer program. That this should be the case in such a crucial emerging business area was considered a serious problem, which was why an initiative was launched to shed some light on the matter and solve the problem.

As group HR director Bill Massey explained to Martha Weird,

> «We need to identify tomorrow's managers in the technology field and start to develop them now. The technology division is considered key to the group's success, but we're not seeing any technology professionals coming through in the various other talent identification projects the group has under way. None of them seem to excel, but I suspect that the tests give more emphasis to relationship and business skills and so don't exactly help the more technical types to stand out. I'm sure the division has people who have great potential, and we need those people. We need them now, and we'll need them even more in the near future. So we must find out who they are and fast-track their development.»

Martha took this as excellent news for her division, as she too suspected that the existing talent identification projects did not benefit the kind of people she had in her division. In fact, she had been worrying about this issue for some time and had even wondered whether the people in her team were less qualified overall than the rest of the AVI group workforce.

The new initiative could help to correct the imbalance by taking the particular characteristics of the technology division into account in a constructive way, with a view to developing talent. Also, the project would help to justify certain budgets, which was a recurrent concern at the end of each year.

The project was called Technology «Talent Inside» and its objective was defined as follows: «to identify the professionals with the greatest development potential in the technology division and establish actions to promote rapid, personalized development that will allow them to become future managers of the division».

«Talent Inside», as it came to be known colloquially, consisted broadly speaking of three clearly differentiated phases:

1) Identification and shortlisting of a group of around thirty people with an excellent track record.

2) Use of development center techniques to identify, within this group, the individuals with the highest potential.

3) Design of a specific plan to develop this group of high-potential individuals. The two-year plan was aimed at accelerating the participants' development and increasing their chances of promotion to positions of greater responsibility.

Phase One: Preparing a Shortlist of Candidates for the «Talent Inside» Project

The preselection phase, carried out during November and December, established strict filters and entry requirements (see **Exhibit 3**). The people who met the requirements represented 0.4% of the division workforce and so constituted something of an elite.

The typical CV of the thirty participants was as follows:

- University degree, mainly in an engineering subject (80% in Computer science and Telecommunications).
- Command of two languages.
- An average of 4.5 years of professional experience, gained entirely in the technology division at AVI, although some (generally the older participants) also had some experience prior to AVI.
- Very good performance assessments in their current positions.
- A clearly articulated desire to change job and grow professionally
- Excellent results in the mental aptitude test.

The preselection phase was international in scope and the results highlighted how the company had expanded abroad in recent years. Specifically, the home countries of the thirty shortlisted candidates were as follows:

United States: 9

Canada: 7

United Kingdom: 4

Mexico: 3

Argentina:	2
Spain:	2
Peru:	1
Portugal:	1
Sweden:	1

Phase Two: Development Center Sessions

The thirty people who passed the online tests were invited to a one-day development center, at which AVI would conduct a competency diagnosis, with two objectives: to select the best, and to identify their strengths and weaknesses in order to be able to work on them over the next two years.

Three development center sessions were prepared, two with English-speaking participants and one with candidates from non-English-speaking countries, with tests in other languages (mainly Spanish). Despite the cost of bringing candidates from other continents, the sessions were held at group headquarters, so as to make it clear that this was a corporate-level project.

The assessments were carried out using the current competency dictionary, and development center techniques were used to ensure maximum objectivity and equal opportunities and to establish a foundation of self-knowledge and reflection that would provide some orientation for the subsequent development of each individual. AVI was already very familiar with these techniques, thanks to its regular talent identification projects. Six generic competencies from the dictionary were assessed on a rising scale from one to four.

In principle, there was no specific rule as to how many people should pass this second phase of the selection process, although there was a fundamental difference of opinion between group HR and division HR. Group HR thought the process should produce at least eight or ten high-potential candidates, who would be the ones who scored highest in the tests.

HR Division, in contrast, were more in favor of setting minimum scores and allowing only those who met the minimum requirements to join the program, without specifying any fixed number of participants. One of the reasons for this was so as not to discredit what was intended to be a star project by accepting mediocre candidates. Martha Weird went so far as to say that, if necessary, she would rather only two people took part in the program in the first year. This would give the program greater prestige and credibility in subsequent years.

Given that each competency would be assessed on a scale of one to four, Martha Weird proposed two requirements for entry to phase three of the «Talent Inside» project:

- An overall score of at least fifteen.
- No competency with a score of one, as this was an automatic disqualifier.

The opposite possibility also had to be considered: what would happen if too many people met the requirements? Having too large a group in the first year of the program was considered unadvisable. In the end, it was decided that they would wait and see how the group performed and act accordingly.

There was also controversy over the scoring. From its earliest dealings with the division and in all its dealings with the group, the HR consulting firm that was taking part in the project had insisted that competency development should not be seen as a matter of «grades», much less of average competency scores, which could vary and were sometimes even contradictory.

The response of the technology division's HR managers was the same as that of group HR, namely that although it might not be the most appropriate approach methodologically speaking, it was certainly the most practical one for their purposes. They even considered creating a ranking to help make decisions.

Phase Three: Two Years of Fast-Track Development

For participants—whether they were the eight or ten top-scoring candidates or the ones who achieved certain minimum scores—the program would be stimulating, demanding, and enriching.

It would include mentoring, training, networking facilitation and development, temporary assignments (including abroad), and participation in cross-organizational projects (see **Exhibit 5**).

Coaching was also a possibility, depending on individual circumstances, although both group and division HR agreed that it would be best not to exhaust every available development option in the first two years. In all but exceptional cases, Talent Inside participants were expected to be offered coaching after a period of four or five years, by which time they would presumably have matured and be more firmly established as professionals.

The Results

The results of the first development center session were somewhat disappointing. Only one of the ten participants met the proposed minimum requirement, i.e., a total score of fifteen or more, and no scores of one. The disappointment was twofold: not only did just one out of ten candidates make the grade, but the performance of several of the others was rated «very poor», especially by the line managers. «Are these really the best candidates we have, or is there something wrong with the filter?» the evaluators wondered when they came together to discuss their observations. After all, they had come to the event expecting to see the division's top talents in action.

Nevertheless, they decided not to make hasty judgments but to wait and see what happened in the next two sessions. The outcome of the second session was almost identical, with only one outstanding candidate and several very unimpressive performances.

The third session went slightly better: two candidates met the requirements, and the overall performance of the rest of the group was more satisfactory than in either of the first two sessions. After the session the evaluators discussed whether candidate maturity was an issue, as it appeared that some of the best scores had been obtained by the candidates with most experience. There was some discussion as to whether there should be a downward correction factor for experience. It was concluded that the observed results added merit to the less experienced participants who scored highly but that it would not be appropriate to apply a correction factor that would distort the overall «picture» of the group (see **Exhibit 6**).

The final results, however, were worrying. Only four candidates met the preset requirements, two of them from countries in which the company was expanding. Martha and her team faced a dilemma: should they put forward only these four candidates, or was it better to lower the standard and select the minimum of eight participants that group HR wanted?

In the end, Martha won the argument with group HR and only the four highest-scoring candidates were chosen to go forward to the development phase of the first «Talent Inside» program. The argument was particularly bitter over the case of Mark Dillon, who was rejected despite having a high overall score, because he did not meet the requirement of having no competencies with a score of one.

As planned, the thirty participants were divided into three categories:

- «Stars»: move on to «Talent Inside».
- «Reserves»: do not move on to the next phase but can try again next time. It would be important to ensure that appropriate training measures were taken to help them succeed in the future.

- «Backstops»: do not move on to the next phase. Their contribution is valued, but they are considered not to have great development potential (average overall score below 12, or scores of one in more than one competency). Future development actions for this group would be targeted at job-specific performance.

The very next day, before the results had been announced, Martha Weird's telephone rang. It was Bill Massey, quite irate. Someone in his team had detected that not all the candidates who had been invited to take part in the development center sessions met the initial requirements. After a quick investigation, it turned out that the human resources business partner of the Europe division had misinterpreted the experience requirement to mean not more than eight years' experience in AVI, when in fact the limit was not more than eight years' experience in total. As a result, candidates had been accepted who should not even have been allowed to take part in the online tests. Although in some cases it was a matter of just a few months, in others the limit was exceeded by two years or more.

The worrying thing was not so much the number of people concerned as their position in the ranking: positions two (Jorge Costa), eleven, twelve and eighteen. Bill and Martha had to quickly decide what to do about them. They considered three options: do nothing; reduce these people's scores and transfer them to the «Backstops» group; or tell them that there had been a mistake and that they should never have taken part and so were excluded, thus making the decision public. There was some question as to whether these people had been aware that they had been selected by mistake, although both Bill and Martha were inclined to think not.

The moment Martha put the phone down, it rang again. It was Sandra, the technology division's business partner for talent development. She was calling to tell Martha that Louis Stevenson, the number one in the «Talent Inside» ranking, had informed her that he was leaving the company because he had accepted a very attractive offer from another company that had promised to meet development expectations that had not been met at AVI. Following standard separation policies, Sandra had arranged an exit interview for the next day. In the circumstances, however, she thought her boss would want to be kept in the picture. She was hesitating whether to tell Louis about the development center results and the new plans the company had for him. But she had encouraged him not to rush into anything and to give himself a chance to discuss the issue at the next day's meeting, to which he had replied that he would be delighted to talk about anything she liked but that he had already given the other company his word.

The Decisions on the Table

As she listened to what Sandra had to say, Martha was assailed by doubts. She suddenly found herself facing the prospect of losing her two top performers. In fact, the whole process could be discredited.

The «chosen few» might turn out to be just two people: Anne Dwight and Luis Rodrigo.

Would it help if she took part in the exit interview with Louis to try to stop him leaving? She did not like making counter-offers, but this was a particularly delicate case. On the other hand, she also had to bear in mind that, for some time now, Sandra had been asking her to delegate more; and in Sandra's last performance assessment she had promised to do so.

She also wondered whether it had been a mistake to insist on applying her own criteria of excellence. If she had followed group HR's advice and chosen the eight or ten top performers, she would not be in this situation now. Was it too late to reconsider the selection criteria?

And what should she do about Jorge Costa and the other people from the Europe division? If they were disqualified and everyone else moved up in the scale, selecting the top eight or ten would mean including positions thirteen and fourteen—well below the level of excellence she had hoped for. But if they were not disqualified, there were other drawbacks, especially for Martha's relationship with headquarters and her personal credibility.

There was also no denying that the poor performance of the «top thirty» at the development center called the whole preselection process into question; and the mix-up over the Europe division candidates hardly helped dispel doubts in that regard. Was the division really so poor in talent? Had they used the right selection filters? How could the age/experience criterion be tied in with the whole issue of detecting potential?

As she wrestled with these thoughts, Martha was reminded of the feelings she had had after many of the leadership and high potential conferences and seminars she had attended. If the aim was to develop potential, it seemed obvious that it was best to start early, with young people who did not have much experience. After all, that was what «potential» was basically about. But was there a limit in the other direction? Was there an age beyond which this kind of initiative was pointless? If so, what age? How could you apply strict quantitative limits in such a fundamental area? Many years' experience of managing people had taught her that everyone is different and does things at a different pace, but also that there have to be rules and standards that cannot be accused of being arbitrary.

EXHIBIT

EXHIBIT 1
Employees and International Presence

	1990	1995	2000	2005	2010
United States	9,927	9,732	10,654	12,114	14,125
Canada	1,227	4,285	5,234	7,287	9,006
South America	25	183	6,391	8,102	10,986
Europe	0	41	2,576	3,934	8,124
Total	11,179	14,141	24,855	31,437	42,241

Source: American Valley annual report.

EXHIBIT 2
Income Statements for Fiscal Years 2006 to 2010
(in millions of dollars)

Income statement	2006	2007	2008	2009	2010
Premiums written and accepted	12,132	13,12	14,773	17,166	18,728
– Non-Life	9,361	10,144	11,152	13,069	14,28
– Life	2,771	2,976	3,622	4,097	4,448
Non-life result	871	1,154	1,365	1,379	1,359
Life result	176	233	265	281	376
Other businesses	42	26	2	–15	–28
Income before tax	1,089	1,413	1,632	1,645	1,707
Net income	549	732	877	1,081	1,094

Source: American Valley annual report.

EXHIBIT 3

Phase One: Preselection

a) Initial population: 8,000 people—all the employees of all the technology companies—would be eligible to sign up to the selection process via the group intranet.

b) «Hard profile» requirements:

b.1)   University degree.

b.2)   Second language (English or Spanish certified to a high level).

b.3)   There was some degree of consensus across business areas and in HR as to the need to set an age limit of 30. But there was a problem: for legal reasons the company was not allowed to include an age requirement in the call for applications. Accordingly, the age requirement was expressed in terms of length of service, setting a maximum of eight years' service.

b.4)   A minimum of two years' service at AVI.

b.5)   Excellent scores («OS» or «VG») in the last three years' performance assessments[2].

b.6)   A willingness to move: given that participating in the development program would require geographic and functional mobility, it was emphasized that participation was voluntary.

As AVI was a young company that had been recruiting a certain type of candidate, a total of 3,800 people met the first three requirements, while 2,000 met the first four. Adding in the fifth requirement reduced the total to 700. Finally, 410 also met the sixth requirement and so were admitted to the selection process for the «Talent Inside» project.

c) Online aptitude tests:

c.1)   Language test.

c.2)   Verbal reasoning test.

c.3)   Numerical reasoning test.

c.4)   Spatial reasoning test.

c.5)   Abstract reasoning test.

---

2. The annual performance assessments were on a scale of five: NI (*needs to improve*), GS (*generally satisfactory*, G (*good*), VG (*very good*) and OS (*outstanding*).

These tests were intended to serve as fair and objective filters for language skills and mental resources. There was some debate over the need to include a test for specific knowledge of the company's business, but the final decision was not to do so, on the grounds that what the company was looking for was (undisclosed) future potential. Each of the five tests was scored on a standardized scale. The overall score was the average of the five test scores, with the added requirement of not scoring below the seventieth percentile in any one test. To reduce the risk of impersonation in the tests, a password administrator was responsible for giving each employee a password at a specific date and time, and the tests had to be completed from each employee's assigned workstation. Of the 410 people who completed the tests, the thirty with the highest average overall score were chosen to go through to the next stage. These thirty had average scores above the ninetieth percentile of the group as a whole.

EXHIBIT 4

Phase Two: The Development Center

The development center sessions were conducted with the help of a specialized consulting firm that was regularly used to provide an independent and experienced opinion on matters of employee development. Three sessions were held, each involving ten candidates and ten evaluators, including consultants, technology division HR professionals, and division line managers.

Six competencies were chosen for analysis, namely, results orientation, customer orientation, leadership, analytical thinking, cooperation, and communication. Each competency was defined and broken down into standardized behaviors that could be assessed on a scale of one to four, four being high.

The techniques used in the development sessions were: group exercise, role play, interview, business case analysis and presentation, and personality test. As was customary, matrices of competencies/tests and candidates/observers were drawn up to ensure that each competency was assessed using more than one test and that each candidate was assessed by more than one observer.

Once the session with the participants was over, the evaluators had another session among themselves in which they analyzed and discussed their observations on each participant.

EXHIBIT 5

Actions Planned for the Third Phase:
Two Years of Fast-Track Development

Mentoring

The «Talent Inside» participants could choose a mentor, who would assist them in their development over the following two years. The mentor would be a member of a preselected group of company managers and would always hold a position at least two levels above that of the participant. No mentor could have more than two mentees. Under the plan, mentors and mentees would meet at least once every two months.

Training

Besides the training decided or already agreed upon with each participant, it was established that each participant would undergo specific training each year, which included the following modules: knowledge of the AVI group, management skills, technical matters, and socioeconomic environment. This training was combined with classroom and online activities.

Networking Facilitation and Development

«Talent Inside» participants would have first right to attend corporate events (both internal and external), as well as certain internal contacts (breakfast with general management, invitations to attend company committees, and «letters of introduction» to other executives in the division or group).

Temporary Assignments

According to the plan, over the two years of the program the participants would work in three different positions, so as to broaden their experience. As a rule, they would spend six months in positions in Spain and one year in the mandatory international assignment.

Participation in Cross-Organizational Projects

Each participant was expected to participate in at least one of these initiatives in each of the two years and would have priority if he/she applied, through the mentor, to take part in more (other duties permitting). Such projects could very often speed up a person's development in areas such as team leadership, account management, visibility to third parties, new business area development, high complexity project management, and strategy.

EXHIBIT 6

Ranking of the Development Center Results

Ranking	Name	Results orientation	Customer orientation	Leadership	Analytical thinking	Coopera-tion	Comunica-tion	Total
1	Louis Stevenson	3	3	3	3	3	3	18
2	Jorge Costa	3	2	3	3	3	2	16
3	Mark Dillon	2	1	4	3	3	3	16
4	Anne Dwight	3	2	2	3	3	2	15
5	Luis Rodrigo	2	2	3	3	2	3	15
6	Caroline Woods	2	2	2	3	3	2	14
7	Alastair Seymour	2	2	3	3	2	2	14
8	Theo Wong	2	2	2	3	3	2	14
9	Paulo Ferreira	2	2	3	3	2	2	14
10	Emiliano Trujillo	2	2	2	2	3	3	14
11	Sara López	2	2	3	2	2	2	13
12	Pedro del Amo	2	2	2	3	2	2	13
13	Emma Petroski	2	2	2	2	2	3	13
14	Sam Walsh	3	3	2	2	2	1	13
15	Philip Brooks	3	3	1	2	2	2	13

Ranking	Name	Results orientation	Customer orientation	Leadership	Analytical thinking	Coopera- tion	Comunica- tion	Total
16	Angela Carina	2	2	2	2	2	2	12
17	Christian Mullin	3	1	2	2	2	2	12
18	Lars Fredriksson	3	2	1	3	1	1	11
19	Gillian Anderton	1	2	2	2	1	2	10
20	Laura Dell	2	1	2	2	1	2	10
21	Laura Vaughan	2	1	1	2	2	2	10
22	Christine Milnar	1	2	1	2	1	2	9
23	David Ferrarini	1	1	2	1	2	2	9
24	Bill Crapilion	2	1	2	2	1	1	9
25	John Peterman	2	2	1	2	1	1	9
26	Pamela Somerset	2	1	1	3	1	1	9
27	Hugh Winters	2	2	1	2	1	1	9
28	Emannuelle Balzer	1	2	1	3	1	1	9
29	Steve Bachelor	2	1	1	2	1	1	8
30	Luciana del Río	1	2	1	2	1	1	8

Third Part

Chapter 10

Leading Means Educating Intelligence and Character

*»Life is always extraordinarily complicated
for someone lacking principles.»*

One characteristic of our era is the lack of reflection and rigor in thinking. Not many people think, and even fewer reason properly, that is, think well in order to act well.

To do this, one must first have the breadth of vision to consider all aspects relevant to the matter and to give each one the correct priority. Secondly, one must have depth, which means becoming familiar with the facts at a precise level of detail. Finally, one must be able to anticipate the foreseeable consequences of actions. In short, thinking well helps us choose the best of all possible actions.

Another feature affecting personal development is that we are living in a social model organized by and for infantilized adults (similar to what is called the «Peter Pan syndrome»), who have been colonized by an adolescence that lasts indefinitely, the outcome of idleness and a lack of effort. One of the causes of this situation, which has never before been seen in human history, is that the entry into adulthood has been delayed by almost a decade, while a second adolescence crops up in adults even more virulently than the first time around.

The Education of Intelligence

The first step consists of restoring a sense of «the imaginative (de finesse),»[1] according to Blaise Pascal, in which each reality is unrepeatable and irreplaceable, and the least replaceable is a person, whose growth begins with education and training. Education requires courage and strength of the person undertaking it, because it makes demands that individuals have to deal with by putting their best foot forward. Intelligence is educated and will is trained; the matter acted upon is knowledge and practical skills; character is strengthened by developing habits that translate into frequently reflective behaviors.

True educational growth – personal and intellectual maturity – is not achieved through noisy activism but through calm reflection, which requires peace and quiet, because to think we must stop to think. The goal is not to be able to do more things, but to become more simply because we are more. Hence the need to somehow be contemplative in the midst of the world, which is not fully met by more or less fashionable substitutes, such as Asian-style meditation practices.

Educating is not equivalent to training or to conveying skills, as something valuable in practice, but to «teaching how to think rigorously and enthusiastically» (A. Llano), so we must overcome the prevailing complacency, characterized by pragmatic shortcuts, the outcome of consumerist bulimia and cultural anorexia.

The important things in life are not taught but are rather learned based on trial and error, an effort that matures and bears fruit only with time and effort. There is no other complete way to deal with a varied and variable reality, which increasingly must be contextualized because it is so short-term and fleeting. What is vital is knowing, learning to know, and learning. Knowledge is a yield that enriches the person who has it; in short, it is a journey that consists of advancing towards our most private selves.

One of the prevailing needs of members of the younger generation – as has happened, with slight differences, to all the generations preceding them, and will continue to happen to those that follow – is to understand what they are and what they truly want. We humans are multifaceted realities that do not allow ourselves to be fully captured by one-dimensional explanations; indeed, true humanism, which is always «new through renewal» in each person, is distinguished by advocating a multidimen-

1. Blaise Pascal. «Discourse on the Passion of Love.» *Minor Works*, edited by Charles W. Eliot, translated by O. W. Wright. Vol. XLVIII, Part 2. The Harvard Classics. New York: P.F. Collier & Son, 1909–14, www.bartleby.com/48/3/.

sional vision both broad and unifying, with a sense of the person and of his or her world.

The steadfast effort to acquire a profound, modern education not based on mere data and slogans, but on criteria and values, as well as on principles that are both strong and adaptable to different life circumstances, is the nontransferable responsibility of each individual. These principles are passed on from generation to generation through coexistence and proximity, and precisely this is the reciprocal influence between parents and children, bosses and subordinates, or colleagues. Permeability requires dialogue, study and reflection, without avoiding the profound dimensions of reality and the questions that point to transcendence. The goal is for each generation to cultivate an attitude and develop life skills, which are totally essential, and furthermore are not passed on without the dedication and effort of the previous generation. Perhaps this has been the most egregious failure since the start of the twenty-first century, and its consequences are now beginning to show.

The youth of every generation have to discover for themselves that the fruitfulness of this attitude of service and effort is more important for them than short-term efficacy or wellbeing. It is the cornerstone of freedom and therefore of creativity, with a sprinkling of sacrifice and effort that have no immediate compensation: «This is how to overcome,» Llano underscores, «that hedonistic immaturity, that infantilism that is at the root of so many educational and sentimental failures.»

For people to develop, it is not enough (although it helps) for them to have fun and avoid useless obstacles. No matter how much technology has progressed, it is worthwhile to deal with difficulties and efforts in order to become what one can become, which is the core of true authenticity. And it is essential to stress the risk of an individual dissolving or dispersing into the infinite identities that computer games or social media offer us. Young people do not need to save their strength, as this is sacrificed for interests them; instead, they need to commit themselves to a meaning that fulfills them as people. Knowledge is only for those who work, that is, for those who think; there is no innate or automatically transferrable knowledge. To know, one has to learn how to know, because knowing and learning are inseparable and are the source and beginning of changes, even if their effective engine is willpower.

Even though all the benefits of the new technologies and their multimedia nature should be harnessed, it is essential to know that they are means and not ends, and that they are useful as long as they are used for something of higher value than themselves and their use. Simply installing or using them does not increase knowledge or happiness. The secret lies in their saving us time while increasing our efficacy, as they help us avoid countless rote tasks, which in turn enables us to devote that time to something that enriches us more as rational beings.

In the knowledge society, and the idle society, the key does not lie in what is known but in knowing, which is the outcome of sustained effort. Creativity and innovation, which are so close to our generation, come from intellectual capacity and emerge from intelligence that is cultivated, not furnished, and perseverant. The important thing is to look out for the future and design it; in all processes of change, the most basic and decisive thing is to get the new direction right, which is not justified by the success achieved but by the ability of achieve a new one.

Education of the Character

«The capacity for suffering defines the quality of a human being,» claimed the German philosopher Friedrich Nietzsche. Even though there is no doubt that pain and its impact should be avoided or mitigated, its presence or the possibility of suffering from it confers seriousness on every person's life. It is a feature that makes us aware that this is real and life is no laughing matter. In no way is the goal to seek it in a pathologically masochistic way, yet nor should we shy away from it, since this robs us of the ability to withstand the adversities that life brings everyone. Tsssssssshe latest generation is not known for its sustained ability to deal with what its members do not like, which is a basic outcome of knowing how to suffer; and it is even less characterized by its ability to manage what is called today – all too easily – frustration. This is a trait with which they have readily infected the subsequent generations they cross paths with. All we have to do is recall the brutal shock of the latest horrible financial crisis, whose consequences are still being felt today, ten years later, by countless millions of people.

One of the keys to good education appears when dealing with what we do not like, what we actively dislike, and even what emotionally destabilizes us or morally confounds us: What to do then? All we have to do is ask the question for the answer to appear: avoiding it is now a life choice that ensures that it will come back again with even more vengeance. Reality stubbornly shows us its harshest side, because it has this side; not wanting to see it only foretells a harder fall; accepting as part of life's landscape, as a travel companion, means gaining realism and therefore a greater likelihood of finding the right response which, just like all appropriate ones, will always be personal and nontransferable. Approaching it as an opportunity to give to others means steeling yourself for the challenge of gaining ground from laziness and idleness. In short, the idea is that dealing with reality helps one grow in experience and common sense.

If we are not prepared to learn the truth of pain and deal with its consequences, we cannot act with full freedom. This is an essential connection.

Ethical Instinct: The Nobility of Feelings

Where this is at stake is in setting the right objectives for ourselves more than in attaining them. To achieve a happy life, or, as Aristotle said, an accomplished life, emotions and feelings play a role that cannot be replaced by intelligence and knowledge, since they provide us with a kind of orientation as to what is good and bad.

In fact, both help us interpret complex situations that facts present as undefined, and they do so with a kind of anticipation, penetration and immediacy that are beyond the intellect; they bring what is called «innate knowledge» or «empathy.» They act as seismographs more than intelligence does, although intelligence then kicks in to provide the essential approach to properly interpret what has been felt. Intelligence without feelings is empty; feelings without intelligence are blind.

Virtues, which shape intelligence and will, are not skills or abilities. They are also not innate but instead acquired through repeated exercise. Young people are not sincere just because they are young, nor are the old wise just because they are old. As Aristotle noted in the *Nicomachean Ethics*,

> «to know what we have to do, we have to do what we want to know... We do not acquire feelings by looking or hearing many times but the opposite. We use them because we have them; we don't have them because we have used them. In contrast, we acquire virtues through prior exercise, and not individually but in a community.»

When one is not yet good, one must act good through an education made of lessons, good examples, reproaches and rectifications; in fact, the proper decisions and actions are ones that have been corrected. When there are no norms for how to apply the rules, an almost intuitive knowledge of the specific situation and the implied ethical requirements is needed. Our decisions are not always completely supported by explicit, formal knowledge; hence moral experience is largely experimental: in human action, the need to decide outstrips the possibilities of knowing.

Choice or decision, according to Aristotle, consists of «the cooperation between a knowledge that one does not know and a wanting to know what one does not know.» In short, man is an *intelligent desire*; hence, it is essential to work on both anthropological elements. Decision points to an action which always, simultaneously and inseparably takes place and translates into a specific commitment and effort every time. An ethical instinct is built upon these moral efforts: a noble person is one who finds good good and therefore likes it. We all can, and therefore should, grow in nobility.

The decision includes a righteous tendency, because it has been corrected, and true knowledge to reflect reality. The success of one's own life is not innate but acquired; it is not inherited but achieved; it is not etched on our foreheads but the result of effort. We all face the alternatives of joy and tragedy, which should not hold back our children or those who depend on us, but instead we should teach them how to deal with them, as Rudyard Kipling recommended.

Happiness is «the best, the most beautiful, the most pleasant» (*Nicomachean Ethics*); everything else is a means or an instrument which is not happiness, but without which it cannot be achieved. One cannot live a mean-spirited or friendless life and be totally happy. Nonetheless, the sobriety induced in a young person – and in the not-so-young as well – by not having enough money will help them value people over things. Happiness is not something achieved just by looking for it, like comfort or pleasure, but a life's yield achieved only through the wise effort of an entire existence.

A happy person has a fortitude which is neither inconstant nor variable, which the misfortunes, ups and downs, and disappointments that are inseparable from human life may erode but will not destroy. It helps the person face the only thing that humans cannot change, namely the absolutely singular reality that is death.

A Note on Success

The trend in favor of high-performance talent, winners' success, and the zeal to be more or to win at all costs cloud a perennial truth. The fact that it has been forgotten lies at the core of the personal, moral, social, and business pathologies we suffer from. We must all hear it, millennials included: **The most important thing is not to be the best, but to be good.**

Bibliography

Andert, D. (2011). Alternating leadership as a proactive organizational intervention: addressing the needs of the baby boomers, generation xers and millennials. Journal Of Leadership, Accountability & Ethics, 8(4), 67-83.

Bannon, S., Ford, K., & Meltzer, L. (2011). Understanding Millennials in the Workplace. CPA Journal, 81(11), 61-65.

Barley, S. R., Meyerson, D. E., & Grodal, S. 2011. Email as a source and symbol of stress. Organization Science, 22: 887–906.

Bauerlein, M. (2009), *The Dumbest Generation: How the Digital Age Stupefies Young Americans and Jeopardizes Our Future (or, Don't Trust Anyone Under 30)*, Penguin Random House, Nueva York.

BBVA (2016), «How to connect with Millennials».

BBVA Innovation Center (2015), «Serie Innovation Trends: Generación Millennial».

Behrens, W. (2009). Managing millennials: They're coming to a workplace near you. Marketing Health Services, 29(1), 19-21.

Birkinshaw, J., & Gibson, C. (2004). Building ambidexterity into an organization. MIT Sloan Management Review, 45, 47-55.

Boehle, S. (2009). Millennial mentors. Training, 46(6), 34-36.

Boswell, W. R., & Olson-Buchanan, J. B. 2007. The use of communication technologies after hours: The role of work attitudes and work–life conflict. Journal of Management, 33: 592–610.

Brown, T., & Martin, R. L. 2015, September. Design for action: How to use design thinking to make great things actually happen. Harvard Business Review: 56–64.

Burstein, David D. (2013). Fast Future: How the Millennial Generation is Shaping Our World. Boston: Beacon Press.

Cahill, T. F., & Sedrak, M. (2012). Leading a Multigenerational Workforce: Strategies for Attracting and Retaining Millennials. Frontiers Of Health Services Management, 29(1), 3-15

Calo, T. (2008). Talent management in the era of the aging workforce: The critical role of knowledge transfer. Public Personnel Management, 37(4), 403-416.

Cambridge University Press e IPSOS (2015), «Cambridge Monitor 3: Millennials en España».

Caraher, Lee. (2015). Millennials & Management: The Essential Guide to Making It Work at Work. Brookline: Bibliomotion, Inc.

Chaudhuri, S., & Ghosh, R. (2012). Reverse mentoring: A social exchange tool for keeping the Boomers engaged and Millennials committed. Human Resource Development Review, 11(1), 55-76. doi: 10.1177/1534484311417562

Cisco (2008) Data leakage worldwide: Common risks and mistakes employees make (White paper). Available at http://www.cisco.com/en/US/solutions/collateral/ns170/ns896/ns895/white_paper_c11-499060.html.   Accessed April 04, 2017.

Cisco Corporation. (2011). 2011 Cisco connected world technology report. Retrieved February 27, 2016, from http://www. cisco.com/c/en/us/solutions/enterprise/connected world-technology-report/index.html#~2011

Colbert, A., Yee, N., & George, G. (2016). The digital workforce and the workplace of the future. Academy of Management Journal. 59 (3), p731-739

De Vita, E. (2015). How banning technology can boost focus and productivity. Financial Times. Retrieved March 24, 2016, from https://www.ft.com/content/ec13e0fe-8897-11e5-90de-f44762bf9896

Deal, J., Altman, D., & Rogelberg, S. (2010). Millennials at work: what we know and what we need to do (if anything). Journal of Business & Psychology, 25(2), 191-199.

Deloitte (2016), «The 2016 Deloitte Millennial Survey. Winning over the next generation of leaders».

Dunbar, R. (2011) How many «Friends» can you really have? IEEE Spectrum. Jun2011, Vol. 48 (6)

Ferri-Reed, J. (2014). Millennializing the workplace. The Journal for Quality & Participation, 37(1), 13-14.

García Lombardía, P., J. R. Pin y G. Stein, DI-753, «Políticas para dirigir a los nuevos profesionales. Motivaciones y valores de la Generación Y», IESE Business School, mayo de 2008.

Gartner. 2011. Gartner predicts over 70 percent of Global 2000 organisations will have at least one gamified application by 2014 [Press release]. Available at http://www.gartner.com/newsroom/id/1844115. Accessed April 04, 2017.

Gesell, I. (2010). How to lead when the generation gap becomes your everyday reality. The Journal for Quality &Participation, 32(4), 21-24.

Gibson, J. W., Greenwood, R., & Murphy, E. F. (2009) Generational differences in the workplace: Personal values, behaviors, and popular beliefs. Journal of Diversity Management 4(3), 1-7.

Gibson, W. J., Greenwood, R. A., & Murphy, E. F. (2010). Analyzing Generational Values among Managers and Non-Managers for Sustainable Organizational Effectiveness. SAM Advanced Management Journal, Winter, 33-43.

Gilson, L. L., Maynard, M. T., Young, N. C. J., Vartiainen, M., & Hakonen, M. 2015. Virtual teams research: 10 years, 10 themes, and 10 opportunities. Journal of Management, 41: 1313–1337.

Glen, R., Suciu, C., & Baughn, C. 2014. The need for design thinking in business schools. Academy of Management Learning & Education, 13: 653–667.

Global Entrepreneurship Research Association, London Business School (2015), «Global Entrepreneurship Monitor».

Goldman Sachs (2016), «Millennial coming on age».

Gonzales, A. L.,&Hancock, J. T. 2011. Mirror, mirror on my Facebook wall: Effects of exposure to Facebook on self-esteem. Cyberpsychology, Behavior, and Social Networking, 14: 79–83.

Goldman Sachs (2016), «Millennials: Coming of Age».

Guha, A. (2010). Motivators and hygiene factors of Generation X and Generation Y-the test of two-factor theory. Vilakshan: The XIMB Journal Of Management, 7(2), 121-132.

Gursoy, D., Maier, T. A., & Chi, C. G. (2008). Generational differences: An examination of work values and generational gaps in the hospitality workforce. International Journal of Hospitality Management, 27(3), 448– 458.

Hall, A. & Stephen, F. (2016). Exploring the workplace communication preferences of millennials. Journal of Organizational Culture, Communications and Conflict 20 (1), 35-44.

Hauw, S., & Vos, A. (2010). Millennials' career perspective and psychological contract expectations: does the recession lead to lowered expectations? Journal of Business & Psychology, 25(2), 293-302.

Hershatter, A., & Epstein, M. (2010). Millennials and the World of Work: An Organization and Management Perspective. Journal of Business & Psychology, 25(2), 211-223.

Hewlett, S.A., Sherbin, L, & Sumberg, K. (2009, July-August). How Gen Y and Boomers will reshape your agenda. Harvard Business Review. Retrieved from https://hbr.org/2009/07/how-gen-y-boomers-will-reshape-youragenda

Ipsos MediaCT & Wikia. 2013, 18 March. Generation Z: A look at the technology and media habits of today's teens. Available at http://www.wikia.com/ Generation_ Z:_A_Look_at_the_Technology_and_Media_Habits_of_Today%E2%80%99s_Teens. Accessed April 04, 2017.

Jong, J. P. & Hartog, D. N. (2007). How leaders influence employees' innovative behaviour, European Journal of Innovation Management, 10(1), 41 – 64.

Kaifi, B. A., Nafei, W. A., Khanfar, N. M., & Kaifi, M. M. (2012). A multi-generational workforce: managing and understanding millennials. International Journal of Business & Management, 7(24), 88-93.

Kelsey, C. (2007), Generation MySpace: Helping Your Teen Survive Online Adolescence, Marlowe & Company, Nueva York.

Konrath, S. H., O'Brien, E. H., & Hsing, C. 2011. Changes in dispositional empathy in American college students over time. Personality and Social Psychology Review, 15: 180–193.

Kowske, B., Rasch, R., & Wiley, J. (2010). Millennials' (lack of) attitude problem: an empirical examination of generational effects on work attitudes. Journal of Business & Psychology, 25(2), 265-279.

Lara, S. y Naval, C. (2010) U. de Navarra «Participación en la sociedad del conocimiento y redes sociales»

Lavezzolo, S.E. & Rodríguez-Lluesma, C. (2015). «La organización matricial: Aspectos básicos, problemas, competencias y herramientas». IESE Publishing, Madrid.

Martensen, A. & Dahlgaard, J. J. (1999). Integrating business excellence and innovation management: Developing vision, blueprint, and strategy for innovation in creative and learning organizations. Total Quality Management 10(4/5), 627 – 635.

Martin, C. A. (2005). From high maintenance to high productivity: What managers need to know about Generation Y. Industrial and Commercial Training, 37(1), 39—44.

McNichols, D. (2010). Optimal knowledge transfer methods: a Generation X perspective, Journal of Knowledge Management, 14(1), 24 – 37.

Michael Page (2016) «Millennials: Amigos o enemigos».

Moon, T. (2014). Mentoring the Next Generation for Innovation in Today's Organization. Journal of Strategic Leadership,5(1),23–35.Retrieved from: http://www.regent.edu/acad/global/publications/jsl/vol5iss1/fullvol5iss1.pdfMoreno, Almudena (2017). Woodman, Daniel (2017)

Myers, K. K., & Sadaghiani, K. (2010). Millennials in the Workplace: A Communication Perspective on Millennials' Organizational Relationships and Performance. Journal of Business & Psychology, 25(2), 225- 238.

Nass,C. (Interviewee) 2013,10May.The myth of multitasking [Interview transcript]. Talk of the Nation, National Public Radio. Available at http://www.npr.org/2013/05/10/182861382/the-myth-of-multitasking. Accessed April 04, 2017.

Nielsen (2014), «Millennials - Breaking the myths».

OCDE (2015), «El bienestar de los estudiantes: resultados de PISA 2015».

Patterson, C. (2005, January). Generational diversity: Implications for consultation and teamwork. Paper presented at the meeting of the Council of Directors of School Psychology Programs on generational differences, Deerfield Beach, FL.

Pérez López, J.A. (1993). Fundamentos de la dirección de empresas, Rialp, Madrid.

Perlow, L. A. 2012. Sleeping with your smartphone: How to break the 24/7 habit and change the way you work. Boston, MA: Harvard Business School Press.

Pfeffer, J (2013).You're still the same: Why theories of power hold over time and across contexts. The Academy at Management Perspectives. 27 (4), 289-280.

Prensky, M. 2001. Digital natives, digital immigrants. On the Horizon, 9(5): 1–6.

PwC (2013). PwC's NextGen: A global gen-erational study. Retrieved January 7, 2016, from http://www. PwC.com/us/en/people-management/publications/ assets/ PwC-nextgen-summary-of-findings.pdf

PwC (2014), «Engaging and empowering Millennials».

Rexrode, C. (2016, March 16). Citigroup to millennial bankers: Take a year off. The Wall Street Journal. Retrieved from http://www.wsj.com/articles/ to-entice-millennial-bankers   citigroup-serves-up-new-perk-take-a-year-off-1458120603

Robson, K., Plangger, K., Kietzmann, J. H., McCarthy, I., & Pitt, L. 2015. Is it all a game? Understanding the principles of gamification. Business Horizons, 58: 411–420.

Schullery, N. M. (2013). Workplace engagement and generational differences in values. Business Communication Quarterly, 76(2), 252-265. doi: 10.1177/1080569913476543

Scott, N. (2014, July). Ambidextrous Strategies and Innovation Priorities: Priming the Pump for Continual Innovation. Technology Innovation Management Review. Retrieved from http://timreview.ca/article/812

Skowronski, M. (2012), «When the bored behave badly (or exceptionally)», Personnel Review, Vol. 41 No. 2, pp. 143-159.

Stein, G. (2016). 9 pautas para gestionar el talento millennial. IESE Insight

Stein, G., Mesa, R. y Martín, M. (2016) DPON-0130 «El liderazgo de los millennials. Rasgos de una generación».

Stein, G., Mesa, R. y Martín, M. (2016) DPON-0131 «Los millennials, el trabajo y la empresa: políticas de gestión y estilos de liderazgo».

Stein, G. y Martín, M. (2016) DPON-0138 «Los millennials y la tecnología».

Stein, J. (2013), «Millennials: The Me Me Me Generation. Why millennials will save us all», TIME, 181(19), pp. 26-34.

Stevens, R. (2010, July). Managing human capital: How to use knowledge management to transfer knowledge to today's multi-generational workforce. International Business Research. 3(3). Retrieved from http://www.ccsenet.org/ journal/index.php/ibr/article/view/6507/5123 Super (1970)

Stewart, J., Goad, O.E., Cavens, K., & Oishi, Shigehiro (2017). Managing millennials: Embracing generational differences.

Tapscott, D. (2009). Grown up digital: How the net generation is changing your world. New York, NY: McGraw-Hill.

Telefónica (2016), «Telefónica Global Millennial Survey. Global Results».

The cocktail analysis y Arena Media (2016), «Observatorio Redes Sociales - Millennials».

Thompson, C. & Gregory, J. B. (2012). Managing Millennials: A framework for improving attraction, motivation, and retention. The Psychologist-Manager Journal, 15(4), 237 - 246.

Travis J.S., & Nichols, T. (2015). Understanding the Millennial Generation. Journal of Business Diversity 15(1), 39-47

Tulgan, B. (2009). Not everyone gets a trophy: How to manage Generation Y. San Francisco, CA: Jossey-Bass.

Turkle, S. 2015. Reclaiming conversation: The power of talk in a digital age. New York, NY: Penguin Press.

Twenge, Jean (2017), «iGen: por qué los chicos superconectados están creciendo menos rebeldes, más tolerantes, menos felices y completamente inmaduros».

Vinichenko, Melnichuk, Kirillov, Makushkin, y Melnichuk (2016). Modern views on the gamification of business

Winograd, M. & Hais, M. (2014, May). How Millennials Could Upend Wall Street and Corporate America. The Initiative on 21st Century Capitalism, 17. Retrieved from http://www.brookings.edu/research/papers/2014/05/millenials-upend-wall-street-corporate-americawinograd-hais

EMPRESA Y ORGANIZACIONES

LIBROS IESE

F. K. Foulkes
Para un trabajo más satisfactorio (agotado)

A. P. Sloan
Mis años en la General Motors (agotado)

B. Roig
La empresa ante las realidades de fin de siglo (agotado)

D. Melé (Coord.)
(Conversaciones sobre Ética Empresarial y Económica)
Ética, mercado y negocios
Ética, trabajo y empleo
Ética en el gobierno de la empresa (1.ª reimpr.)
Ética en la actividad financiera (2.ª ed.)
Ética en dirección comercial y publicidad
Consideraciones éticas sobre la iniciativa emprededora y la empresa familiar
Raíces éticas del liderazgo
Conciliar trabajo y familia: un reto para el siglo XXI

J. M.ª Rodríguez Porras
El factor humano en la empresa. Apuntes

Instituto de Empresa y Humanismo (editor)
Capitalismo y cultura cristiana

J. Riverola, B. Cuadrado
Arte y oficio de la simulación. Un entorno completo y su uso en la mejora de los servicios

S. Gómez López-Egea
La retribución y la carrera profesional: teoría y práctica (2.ª ed.)

P. Cardona, P. García-Lombardía
Cómo desarrollar las competencias de liderazgo (5.ª ed.)
How to develop leadership competencies

B. O'C. Leggett
Developing your persuasive edge. The key to your communication success in business

M. Á. Gallo
Ideas básicas para dirigir la empresa familiar (2.ª ed.)

N. Chinchilla y M. Moragas
Masters of our destiny (2.ª ed.)

P. Cardona y H. Wilkinson
Creciendo como líder (2.ª ed.)

E. Suárez Ruz
Tendencias en la dirección de personas: de la flexibilidad a la flexiguridad

B. Muñoz-Seca y J. Riverola (Eds.)
Arte y eficiencia. El sector de la cultura visto desde la empresa

IPD. José Luis Suárez (Coord.)
La inversión Inmobiliaria en España 2001-2011. 10 años de IPD en España

B. O'C. Leggett
The Little Book of Rhetoric: Soft Power

I. Olivares, K. Kase, G. Stein, J.R. Pin, E. Carretero
Han Feizi. Filosofía de dirección y estrategia

M.Á. Gallo, G. Gómez
Evolución y desarrollo de la empresa y de la familia: marcos para oficinas de familia

L.M. Calleja
Gobierno institucional. La dirección colegiada

F. Pereira y M.ª J. Grandes
Dirección y contabilidad financiera (1.ª reimpresión)

J. R. Pin Arboledas y Guido Stein
Claves de la negociación colectiva. De la teoría a la realidad

Guido Stein
Líderes y *Millennials*. Un *meeting point* de generaciones (2.ª ed.)

Guido Stein
Leaders and Millennials. A Meeting Point of Generations

MANUALES IESE

F. Pereira, E. Ballarín, J. M.ª Rosanas, M.ª Jesús Grandes
Contabilidad para dirección (25.ª ed.)

G. W. Plossl, O. W. Wight
El control de la producción y los stocks

G. A. Steiner
Planificación de la alta dirección
Tomo I (4.ª ed.)
Tomo II (4.ª ed.)

A. Valero y Vicente, J. L. Lucas
Política de empresa (8.ª ed.)

J. Farrán
Comercialización agroalimentaria

B. O'C. Leggett
Comunicación oral en la empresa

P. Fernández, J. Santomá
Finanzas para directivos (2.ª ed.)

J. Farrán, A. Agustín, J. C. Yábar, J. M. Rizo, R. Lacasta, J. Ireland
Distribución y logística

A. Valero y Vicente, E. Taracena Figueroa
La empresa de negocios y la alta dirección (2.ª ed.)

P. Agell y J. A. Segarra
Escuchando la voz del mercado. Decisiones de segmentación y posicionamiento

C. Chiesa de Negri
Fidelizando para fidelizar. Cómo dirigir, organizar y retener a nuestro Equipo Comercial (4.ª ed.)